COUNTRIES, REGIONAL STUDIES, TRADING BLOCKS, UNIONS, WORLD ORGANIZATIONS

REPUBLIC OF THE PHILIPPINES AND U. S. RELATIONS

COUNTRIES, REGIONAL STUDIES, TRADING BLOCKS, UNIONS, WORLD ORGANIZATIONS

Additional books in this series can be found on Nova's website under the Series tab.

Additional E-books in this series can be found on Nova's website under the E-books tab.

COUNTRIES, REGIONAL STUDIES, TRADING BLOCKS, UNIONS, WORLD ORGANIZATIONS

REPUBLIC OF THE PHILIPPINES AND U. S. RELATIONS

MARGARET R. VOIGT
EDITOR

Nova Science Publishers, Inc.
New York

For permission to use material from this book please contact us:
Telephone 631-231-7269; Fax 631-231-8175
Web Site: http://www.novapublishers.com

LIBRARY OF CONGRESS CATALOGING-IN-PUBLICATION DATA

Republic of the Philippines and U.S. relations / editor, Margaret R. Voigt.
p. cm.
Includes index.
ISBN 978-1-61668-951-3 (softcover)
1. United States--Relations--Philippines. 2.
Philippines--Relations--United States. I. Voigt, Margaret R.
E183.8.P5R47 2010
327.730599--dc22
2010025655

Published by Nova Science Publishers, Inc. ✦ New York

CONTENTS

PREFACE

This book focuses on the current state of the United States and the Republic of the Philippines relations. The U.S. and Philippines maintain close ties based upon historical relations, common interests, shared values, and the large Filipino-American population. Major U.S. policy objectives in the Philippines include bolstering the Philippines as a strong U.S. ally in Southeast Asia, assisting the Armed Forces of the Philippines (AFP) in counterterrorism efforts, supporting the peace process in Mindanao, as well as helping the AFP to modernize its equipment and adhere to democratic principles and providing assistance for political and economic development.

Chapter 1 - The United States and the Republic of the Philippines (RP) maintain close ties based upon historical relations, common interests, shared values, and the large Filipino-American population. Although the United States closed its military bases in the Philippines in 1992, bilateral military cooperation resumed following territorial disputes between the Philippines and China in 1994 and the launching of the Global War on Terrorism in 2002. Major U.S. policy objectives in the Philippines include: bolstering the Philippines as a strong U.S. ally in Southeast Asia; assisting the Armed Forces of the Philippines (AFP) in counterterrorism efforts; supporting the peace process in Mindanao; helping the AFP to modernize its equipment and adhere to democratic principles; and providing assistance for political and economic development. Since 2001, the Philippines has received the most dramatic increases in U.S. foreign aid in Southeast Asia, largely for counterterrorism purposes, including not only military assistance but also health, education, and economic assistance in Mindanao.

The Philippines faces terrorist threats from several groups, including Jemaah Islamiyah (JI), the main Southeast Asian Islamic terrorist organization with reported ties to Al Qaeda, and Abu Sayyaf, a small, violent Muslim separatist group which operates in the southern Philippines. The Moro Islamic Liberation Front (MILF), a Muslim separatist group with an estimated armed strength of over 10,000, seeks a homeland with a high degree of autonomy in Muslim-majority areas of Mindanao. Since 2002, the United States has provided non-combat assistance in joint military exercises which have helped to significantly reduce the size of Abu Sayyaf. Nonetheless, Abu Sayyaf continues to operate through its growing cooperation with JI and some factions of the MILF. In August 2008, the Philippine government and the MILF signed a Memorandum of Agreement setting up a framework for expanded autonomy in Mindanao. However, Christian politicians from Mindanao filed a suit with the Philippine Supreme Court, which ruled the accord unconstitutional, unleashing a period of fighting between MILF and government forces.

While the United States remains the dominant foreign military, political, economic, and cultural influence in the Philippines, China has become a major—perhaps the largest—source of financing for infrastructure, energy, and agricultural development and arguably has engaged in more active diplomacy. Some U.S. and RP policy makers have expressed concern regarding China's growing "soft power" and the perceived lack of U.S. comprehensive attention to Philippine and regional issues.

The United States has an interest in promoting stable and effective democratic governance in the Philippines. President Gloria Arroyo has faced at least three coup attempts and four impeachment bids. Pervasive official corruption and a wave of politically-motivated killings of mass media personnel and extrajudicial killings of leftists and social activists have created an impression of lawlessness. Two independent investigations into the extrajudicial killings conducted in 2006- 2007 implicated the Philippine Armed Forces.

Chapter 2 - The United States has had a continuous relationship with the Philippine Islands since 1898, when they were acquired by the United States as a result of the Spanish-American War. Filipinos have served in, and with, the U.S. Armed Forces since the Spanish-American War, and especially during World War II. The Islands remained a possession of the United States until 1946.

Since 1946, Congress has passed several laws affecting various categories of Filipino veterans. Many of these laws have been liberalizing laws that have provided Filipino World War II veterans with medical and monetary benefits similar to benefits available to U.S. veterans.

However, not all veterans' benefits are available to veterans of the Commonwealth Army of the Philippines, Recognized Guerrilla Forces, and New Philippine Scouts. In the 110th Congress, two measures, H.R. 760 and S. 57, have been introduced that would eliminate the distinction between the Regular, or "Old," Philippine Scouts and the other three groups of veterans—the Commonwealth Army of the Philippines, Recognized Guerrilla Forces, and New Philippine Scouts—making them all fully eligible for veterans' benefits similar to those received by U.S. veterans.

This chapter defines the four specific groups (Regular Philippine Scouts, Commonwealth Army of the Philippines, Recognized Guerilla Forces, and New Philippine Scouts) of Filipino nationals who served under the command of the United States, outlines the Rescission Acts of 1946, benefit changes since 1946, current benefits for Filipino veterans by group, and recent legislative proposals and legislation, including the American Recovery and Reinvestment Act of 2009 (ARRA, P.L. 111-5).

Chapter 3 features a profile of the Philippines.

In: Republic of the Philippines and U.S. Relations ISBN: 978-1-61668-951-3
Editor: Margaret R. Voigt

Chapter 1

THE REPUBLIC OF THE PHILIPPINES: BACKGROUND AND U.S. RELATIONS*

Thomas Lum and Larry A. Niksch

SUMMARY

The United States and the Republic of the Philippines (RP) maintain close ties based upon historical relations, common interests, shared values, and the large Filipino-American population. Although the United States closed its military bases in the Philippines in 1992, bilateral military cooperation resumed following territorial disputes between the Philippines and China in 1994 and the launching of the Global War on Terrorism in 2002. Major U.S. policy objectives in the Philippines include: bolstering the Philippines as a strong U.S. ally in Southeast Asia; assisting the Armed Forces of the Philippines (AFP) in counterterrorism efforts; supporting the peace process in Mindanao; helping the AFP to modernize its equipment and adhere to democratic principles; and providing assistance for political and economic development. Since 2001, the Philippines has received the most dramatic increases in U.S. foreign aid in Southeast Asia, largely for counterterrorism purposes, including not only military assistance but also health, education, and economic assistance in Mindanao.

* This is an edited, reformatted and augmented version of a CRS Report for Congress publication dated January 2009.

The Philippines faces terrorist threats from several groups, including Jemaah Islamiyah (JI), the main Southeast Asian Islamic terrorist organization with reported ties to Al Qaeda, and Abu Sayyaf, a small, violent Muslim separatist group which operates in the southern Philippines. The Moro Islamic Liberation Front (MILF), a Muslim separatist group with an estimated armed strength of over 10,000, seeks a homeland with a high degree of autonomy in Muslim-majority areas of Mindanao. Since 2002, the United States has provided non-combat assistance in joint military exercises which have helped to significantly reduce the size of Abu Sayyaf. Nonetheless, Abu Sayyaf continues to operate through its growing cooperation with JI and some factions of the MILF. In August 2008, the Philippine government and the MILF signed a Memorandum of Agreement setting up a framework for expanded autonomy in Mindanao. However, Christian politicians from Mindanao filed a suit with the Philippine Supreme Court, which ruled the accord unconstitutional, unleashing a period of fighting between MILF and government forces.

While the United States remains the dominant foreign military, political, economic, and cultural influence in the Philippines, China has become a major—perhaps the largest—source of financing for infrastructure, energy, and agricultural development and arguably has engaged in more active diplomacy. Some U.S. and RP policy makers have expressed concern regarding China's growing "soft power" and the perceived lack of U.S. comprehensive attention to Philippine and regional issues.

The United States has an interest in promoting stable and effective democratic governance in the Philippines. President Gloria Arroyo has faced at least three coup attempts and four impeachment bids. Pervasive official corruption and a wave of politically-motivated killings of mass media personnel and extrajudicial killings of leftists and social activists have created an impression of lawlessness. Two independent investigations into the extrajudicial killings conducted in 2006- 2007 implicated the Philippine Armed Forces.

OVERVIEW

The United States and the Republic of the Philippines (RP) maintain close ties stemming from the U.S. colonial period (1898-1946). Although the United States closed its military bases in the Philippines in 1992 (Subic Naval Base and Clark Air Base), cooperation in counterterrorism efforts has brought the two treaty allies closer together. During President Gloria MacapagalArroyo's state visit to Washington in May 2003, the Bush Administration pledged increased military assistance and designated the Republic of the Philippines as a Major Non-NATO Ally.[1] The main pillars of the bilateral relationship are the U.S.-RP security alliance, counterterrorism cooperation, trade and investment ties, democratic values, and extensive people-to-people contacts. Filipino-Americans number approximately three million, making them the second-largest Asian-American group in the United States, and comprise the largest number of immigrants in the U.S. armed forces. An estimated 250,000 Americans live in the Philippines.[2] Despite general agreement on the importance of U.S.-RP relations and the war on terrorism, bilateral frictions occasionally have arisen as Philippine foreign policy has become more independent and assertive regarding RP sovereignty and self-interests or driven by domestic political pressures. Furthermore, areas of cooperation have narrowed somewhat since 2001. According to some analysts, Manila has begun to define its security needs in a more multilateral rather than bilateral context, while the United States government has been accused of viewing the Philippines and the Southeast Asia region largely through a prism of terrorism.[3]

Policy Issues for Congress

Broad U.S. policy objectives include: maintaining the U.S.-RP alliance; assisting the Armed Forces of the Philippines (AFP) in counterterrorism efforts; supporting the peace process in Mindanao; supporting AFP modernization and administrative reform; promoting broad-based economic growth; and helping the Philippines to develop stable and responsive democratic institutions. The United States may have reached a crossroads where it faces fundamental policy questions regarding its policies toward the Philippines. These include: whether to continue current levels of military and development assistance despite unabated political violence and instability; whether to press for a more aggressive role for U.S. military forces in counterterrorism operations, despite the potential for aggravating tensions in Mindanao and other regions in the south or provoking anti-U.S. sentiment among some groups; and whether to assume a role in the MILF-RP government peace process, despite the lack of a clear outcome.

Some policy makers have questioned the effectiveness of seven years of significantly increased U.S. assistance to the Philippines, which they argue have not fundamentally altered the dynamics of the insurgency in Mindanao and widespread economic disparities and political instability. Other analysts argue that raising funding levels for Foreign Military Financing (FMF), anti-terrorism assistance (NADR), and military training (IMET) to the Philippines would help the AFP to fight terrorist and separatist groups as well as promote democratic principles in the military.

Some observers contend that the United States should pay more attention to the underlying causes of terrorism and separatist insurgency in the Philippines, such as the poverty and official corruption. They advocate increasing funding for U.S. development and other aid programs, especially in Muslim areas of Mindanao, that help provide for economic development, education, government accountability, and conflict mitigation programs. They also support U.S. military involvement in local infrastructure projects (civic action programs).

The United States has an interest in promoting stable and effective democratic governance in the Philippines. While Filipinos enjoy a high degree of civil liberty, political leaders are freely scrutinized, and elections are largely free, corruption, political violence, and the lack of civilian control over the military continue to present major and in some cases growing challenges to Philippine democracy. Politically-motivated acts of violence against journalists and other mass media personalities and extrajudicial killings of individuals linked to leftist groups have risen since Gloria Macapagal-Arroyo assumed the presidency in 2001. The United States government has attempted to help address the problems of corruption and extra-judicial killings largely through its foreign assistance activities. U.S. programs related to political killings include providing additional funding to the Philippine Commission on Human Rights, training Philippine investigators and prosecutors, educating military and law enforcement personnel in the areas of human rights and civil liberties, supporting judicial system improvements, and aiding civil society groups. The Consolidated Appropriations Act for FY2008 placed conditions on a portion of military assistance in order to help compel the RP government to address this issue.

Some Philippine leaders and U.S. policy analysts have called for broader U.S. engagement (beyond counterterrorism cooperation), in part to counter China's growing influence in the RP. The United States is the largest bilateral source of foreign direct investment and the second largest bilateral provider of official development assistance in the RP after Japan. The United States remains the RP's largest trading partner, although bilateral trade contracted slightly in 2007, while RP-China trade continued to expand rapidly. When

Hong Kong is included, however, RP-China/Hong Kong trade now exceeds RP-U.S. trade.[4] In the past few years, China has become a major sponsor of infrastructure, energy, agriculture, and mining development in the Philippines. The RP reportedly is the largest recipient of PRC loans in Southeast Asia. Some observers argue that although most RP leaders do not want Chinese economic assistance to come at the expense of U.S. friendship, Philippine reliance on China may potentially conflict with U.S. priorities in the RP.

Political Developments

Since 2005, President Arroyo has faced popular protests calling for her resignation, at least three coup attempts by elements of the Philippine military, and four impeachment bids (three have failed and a fourth is not expected to prevail). She won the presidential election of 2004 (a nonrenewable six-year term), after having already served for three and one-half years, but subsequently was accused of attempting to rig the election.[5] In October 2008, the President's approval rating stood at 27%, with 54% dissatisfied with her performance.[6] The government's successful fiscal reforms, lack of popular leadership alternatives, support from the top ranks of the military, and relative quiet of the Catholic church of the Philippines, have helped to prevent opposition movements from gathering momentum. Likely top contenders to succeed Arroyo in 2010 include: Vice President Noli de Catro; former Senate President Manuel B. Villar (Nacionalista Party); Senator Loren Legarda (Genuine Opposition coalition), and Senator Manuel "Mar" Roxas II (Liberal Party).[7]

On the one hand, RP citizens enjoy a high level of political freedom, including a robust civil society, while the legislative and judicial branches exert checks upon the presidency. On the other hand, Philippine politics are plagued by corruption and cronyism, and power is concentrated in the hands of entrenched socio-economic elites. One analyst describes the Philippines as a "weak state ... captured by strong interests."[8] Another rising concern among some opposition and civil society groups is the growing influence of the Philippine security forces in the Arroyo Administration, exemplified by the number of armed forces and police officials appointed to high level positions in government. They argue that Arroyo has thereby attempted to bolster her strength both within the military itself and vis-a-vis opposition groups; in return for the military's support, the President has protected the security forces from charges of corruption and human rights abuses.[9] Freedom House characterizes the Philippines as "partly free"—its rating of political rights falling from 3 to 4 (on a scale of 1 to 7) in 2008 due to allegations of corruption and political killings.[10] The Economist Intelligence Unit (EIU) ranks the RP 77th out of 167 countries in terms of democracy, owing largely to ongoing corruption and attempted military coups. However, the EIU scores the Philippines high on the electoral process, pluralism, and civil liberties.[11]

The Philippine legislature acts as a "watchdog" toward the executive branch, but historically has had difficulty articulating and carrying out broad policy options and programs. Political parties and groupings tend to be fragmented and shifting, driven more by individual personality or geographic and sectoral interests than by unifying ideologies, platforms, and policy goals. The public often elects and places its trust in charismatic leaders, who distribute the spoils of victory to their cronies.[12]

2007 Congressional Elections

The May 2007 mid-term elections reportedly were marred by violence, intimidation, fraud, disenfranchisement, and other voting irregularities in some areas, particularly in the south. An estimated 116 people were killed and 121 were wounded in election-related violence.[13] However, according to some observers, the 2007 elections were carried out honestly overall and represented an improvement over the 2004 elections. President Arroyo, whose term ends in 2010, gained support in the lower House following the elections, thus helping her avert another impeachment bid. However, pro-Arroyo parties lost their narrow majority in the Senate. This has made it more difficult for the President to carry out her policy agenda.[14]

Politically-Motivated Violence and Extrajudicial Killings

Politically-motivated acts of violence against journalists and other mass media personalities and extrajudicial killings of individuals linked to leftist groups have risen since Gloria MacapagalArroyo assumed the presidency in 2001, reportedly reaching a peak in 2006. According to one estimate, 58 journalists reportedly have been killed since 2001.[15] Many experts attribute these killings to local power struggles rather than to a systematic crackdown on media freedom directed by Manila. In many cases, powerful, local political families reportedly have targeted journalists or mass media personalities who had either exposed the business practices of these families or threatened their interests by allying with rival families or criticizing local government corruption. The police, often beholden to local elites, have been accused of failing to perform proper investigations, while higher levels of government have been blamed for not aggressively pursuing or prosecuting those responsible for the violence.[16]

The communist insurgency has spawned another type of killing. Since the late 1960s, the Communist Party of the Philippines (CPP) allegedly has developed an extensive array of front groups in rural areas. These groups often have operated in close proximity to non-communist but left-leaning social groups and non-governmental organizations (NGOs) trying to assist poorer Filipinos.[17] Members of both communist groups and civil society have been the targets of assassination. Between 2001 and 2007, hundreds of mostly leftist political, trade union, farmer, church, and human rights activists reportedly were killed (over 800 according to Philippine human rights groups). However, a Philippine National Police task force declared that about three- fourths of these killings were non-political in nature.[18]

Some reports have attributed most of these deaths to the Armed Forces of the Philippines. Experts argue that the AFP has been so dedicated to eradicating the CPP and its armed wing, the New People's Army (NPA), both of which are on the U.S. list of terrorist organizations, that it has cast an excessively wide net over leftist activists and networks. The RP government's February 2006 proclamation of an "all out war" against communist insurgents and other "enemies of the state" gave further license to the AFP's unrestricted campaign against perceived leftist security threats. Many analysts contend that Arroyo has been reluctant to discipline the military, since its top ranks have provided her with much needed political support.[19]

AFP officials have largely rejected the claims that extrajudicial killings have occurred or that the military should be blamed, as well as the notion that the victims were innocent. Some military officials have responded to allegations with counterclaims that the deaths were a fabrication of the CPP, that political and social organizations of whom many alleged victims were members, such as the National Democratic Front, Bayan Muna, and Karapatan, were fronts for the CPP, or that activists were killed as part of a CPP intra-organizational purge.[20]

In 2006, partially in response to outcries from Philippine and international human rights groups, the Catholic Church of the Philippines, and European countries, President Arroyo created a special task force to investigate the extra-judicial killings and invited the United Nations Special Rapporteur on Extrajudicial, Summary or Arbitrary Executions, Philip Alston, to conduct a fact- finding mission. The task force (Melo Commission) and the Special Rapporteur released their findings in January 2007 and February 2007, respectively.[21] Both studies implicated the Philippine armed forces but not the government. They largely rejected the assertions that many leftist activists were linked to the Communist Party, killed by the CPP as part of an internal organizational purge, or died in military combat between the AFP and the New People's Army. In response to recommendations of the Melo Commission and Special Rapporteur, the Arroyo government reportedly has taken major steps to bolster the investigation and prosecution of cases involving unlawful killings and establish procedures to ensure greater accountability in the military and police forces.[22] Although the number of such deaths has declined, some human rights advocates contend that most of the perpetrators of such crimes have remained unpunished.[23]

ECONOMIC CONDITIONS

During the post-World War II period, the Philippines, with its American-influenced political institutions and culture, well-educated and talented workforce, and widespread use of English, was considered by some observers to be the second most-developed country in East Asia, after Japan. However, the country has fallen behind other developing nations in the region. For example, the Philippines has slipped below China both in gross domestic product (GDP) per capita ($3,200 in the Philippines compared to $5,400 in China)[24] and "human development." The United Nations Development Program's Human Development Index (HDI) ranked the Philippines 90th and China 81st for 2007-2008.[25]

Despite these declines, many analysts credit President Arroyo for putting the economy back on a strong footing after several years of stagnation. Arroyo's fiscal reforms, which included reducing public debt through more aggressive collection of taxes, streamlining government operations, and privatizing public sector enterprises, contributed to economic growth. The government budget deficit declined, agriculture, export industries (electronics), and business process outsourcing (BPO) performed well, and remittances from abroad surged. In addition, foreign investment rebounded and the poverty rate declined. The Philippines is the world's second largest center for business process outsourcing, after India, employing 340,000 persons and accounting for 3% of GDP.[26] Real growth in gross domestic product averaged 5% during 2004-2006 and reached 7% in 2007. However, economic growth is expected to slow to 4.3% in 2008 and 1.3% in 2009, due in large part to the slowdown in the global economy. Falling remittances and foreign investment, as well as price inflation, particularly that pertaining to rice and fuel, are likely to act as drags on the economy.[27]

Philippine prosperity is highly dependent upon remittances from abroad. In 2007, roughly 8 million overseas Filipino workers (OFWs) remitted $17 billion, compared to $15.25 billion in 2006, making the RP the fourth largest recipient of remittances worldwide. Remittances constitute over 10% of GDP or more than half the government budget.[28] While this source of income is a boon to the economy, some observers argue that it promotes consumption over long-term investment. Furthermore, the flight of educated professionals represents a brain drain as well as the depletion of the middle class, which has long been considered the bulwark of democracy in the Philippines.

The RP's largest trading partners and foreign investors are the People's Republic of China (PRC), the United States, and Japan. According to RP official data, bilateral trade with China (including Hong Kong) is slightly higher than that with the United States and growing at a faster rate. (See **Table 1**.) The Philippines also benefits from annual trade surpluses with China. The RP exports primarily electrical machinery and natural resources to China and electrical machinery and textiles to the United States.[29]

Table 1. Philippines Bilateral Trade with the United States, China, and Japan, 2007 ($ billions)

	Philippines Data				Trade Partner Data			
	Imports	**Exports**	**Total Trade**	**% Change from 2006**	**Imports**	**Exports**	**Total Trade**	**% Change from 2006**
U.S.	7.9	8.5	16.4	-2	7.7	9.4	17.1	-1
China	4.0	5.7	9.7	16	7.5	23.1	30.6	31.3
Hong Kong	2.2	5.8	8.0	40	2.8	6.3	9.1	13.7
Japan	6.6	7.3	13.9	-5	9.5	8.7	18.2	7.6

Source: Global Trade Atlas.

Note: Philippine and PRC trade data vary significantly.

Promoting U.S. Trade and Investment

Some foreign policy makers advocate trade-liberalization policies that would encourage greater U.S. trade with and investment in the Philippines, which they argue would help promote economic development and social and political stability as well as to counteract growing Chinese influence. The United States has concluded Trade and Investment Framework Agreements (TIFAs) with five major economies in Southeast Asia, including the Philippines. TIFAs provide forums for the discussion and resolution of bilateral trade issues as well as foundations for potential FTA negotiations. In 2006, the United States Trade Representative (USTR) upgraded the RP from "Priority Watch List" to "Watch List" for improvements in its efforts to reduce Intellectual Property Rights (IPR) violations. In June 2008, the two countries signed an Agreement of Cooperation on Agriculture and Related Fields that would allow for the sale of fresh fruits from the Philippines to the United States.[30] Some analysts expect little progress on a U.S.-RP FTA in the foreseeable future, however, due to likely opposition or higher standards imposed upon them in the 111th Congress and under the Obama Administration.[31]

U.S. Foreign Assistance

Since 2001, the Philippines has received the most dramatic increases in U.S. foreign assistance in Southeast Asia. The main goals of U.S. assistance in the Philippines include: fighting terrorism through both military and non-military means; supporting the peace process in Muslim Mindanao; promoting health and education programs, especially in conflict-ridden areas of Mindanao; increasing private sector competitiveness; and promoting good governance. "Peace and Security" efforts, which receive the greatest funding, include assistance for counterterrorism operations, social and economic programs in Mindanao, and the Philippine Defense Reform (PDR) program, the aim of which is to create institutional mechanisms for preventing extra-judicial killings.[32] In 2006, the Millennium Challenge Corporation (MCC) designated the Philippines as a "threshold" country or close to meeting criteria for receiving additional assistance through the Millennium Challenge Account (MCA). The Philippines recently initiated a two-year, $21 million MCA threshold program that focuses on fighting corruption and improving government revenue collection. (See Table 2.)

The Consolidated Appropriations Act for FY2008, Section 699E provided up to $30 million for Foreign Military Financing for the Philippines, of which $2 million would be made available if the U.S. Secretary of State reported that the Philippine government and military were adequately addressing the problem of extra-judicial killings: investigating and prosecuting military personnel and others who had been credibly alleged to have committed extrajudicial executions or other violations of human rights; implementing policies promoting human rights safeguards in the military; and not engaging in acts of intimidation or violence against members of legal organizations who advocate for human rights.

In September 2008, the House and Senate of the U.S. Congress passed a continuing resolution (CR), H.R. 2638 (Consolidated Security, Disaster Assistance, and Continuing Appropriations Act, 2009). The bill was signed into law as P.L. 110-329. The CR for FY2009 continues most foreign operations funding through March 6, 2009, at FY2008 levels.

Table 2. U.S. Assistance to Philippines, 2005-2009 (thousands of dollars)

Account	FY2005	FY2006	FY2007	FY2008 estimate	FY2009 request
CSH	27,050	24,651	24,362	24,967	20,043
DA	27,576	24,212	15,448	27,321	56,703
ESF	30,720	24,750	29,750	27,773	—
FMF	29,760	29,700	39,700	29,757	15,000
IMET	2,915	2,926	2,746	1,475	1,700
INCLE	3,968	1,980	1,900	794	1,150
NADR	2,257	4,968	4,198	4,531	4,625
Peace Corps	2,820	2,767	2,820	2,753	—
Totals	127,066	115,954	120,924	119,371	99,221
Food Aid					
P.L. 480 Title I USDA Loan	20,000	0	0	0	0
FFP	1,720	6,335	3,655	—	—
Section 416(b)	5,644	0	0	—	—

Sources: U.S. Department of State; USAID; U.S. Department of Agriculture.

Key to Foreign Assistance Acronyms

CSH	Child Survival and Health	IMET	International Military Education and Training
DA	Development Assistance	INCLE	International Narcotics Control and Law Enforcement
ESF	Economic Support Funds	NADR	Non-Proliferation, Anti-Terrorism and De-Mining
FMF	Foreign Military Financing	FFP	Food for Progress

TERRORIST, SEPARATIST, AND COMMUNIST MOVEMENTS

The Muslim terrorist and insurgency situation in the southern Philippines has become increasingly complex since 2002, when Philippine and U.S. forces conducted a relatively successful operation against the Abu Sayyaf terrorist group on Basilan island off the southwestern tip of the big southern island of Mindanao.[33] Over a span of about four years, the operation reduced Abu Sayyaf's strength from an estimated 1,000 active fighters to an estimated 200-400.[34] (See Figure 1, Map of the Philippines.) However, there are other developments of a decidedly negative nature that could worsen the overall situation in the southern Philippines and even the Philippines as a whole.

One worrisome trend is the growing cooperation among Abu Sayyaf, several major Moro Islamic Liberation Front (MILF) commands, and elements of Jemaah Islamiyah (JI) on Mindanao. JI, the Southeast Asian Muslim terrorist organization with ties to Al Qaeda, appears to have made Mindanao a primary base for building up its cadre of terrorists. Moreover, this cooperation among the three groups appears to be transforming Mindanao into a significant base of operations rather than just a site for training; and these operations appear to increasingly target the Philippines for terrorist attacks. A related development is the emergence of a group of Filipino Muslim converts in the northern Philippines, the Rajah Solaiman Movement, which is working with Abu Sayyaf and JI. The result has been an increase in terrorist bombings since 2002, both in number and destructiveness, and an increase in the level of bombing targets in the northern Philippines, including Manila. Other obstacles to resolving the conflict in the south include distrust between the MNLF and MILF and the factionalism that exists among the two fronts. Some analysts suggest that if the MILF agrees to a settlement with the government, and ceases to represent a more fundamentalist alternative, then some of the more radical members and leaders may be compelled to join JI or Abu Sayyaf.[35]

The Abu Sayyaf Group

Abu Sayyaf is a small, violent, faction-ridden Muslim group that operates in western Mindanao and on the Sulu islands extending from Mindanao. It has a record of killings and hostage-taking for ransom and has had past, sporadic links with Al Qaeda.[36] In May 2001, Abu Sayyaf kidnapped and took hostage 20 people from a resort on the island of Palawan, including three American citizens. Some of the Filipino hostages were later freed, while one of the Americans, Guillermo Sobero, was beheaded. One year later, in June 2002, Filipino army rangers attempted a rescue in which one of the remaining Americans, Martin Burnham, was killed along with a Filipina hostage. Burnham's wife, Gracia, was freed.

Philippine military operations since 2001, supported by the United States, have weakened Abu Sayyaf on Basilan island and in the Sulu islands. However, under the leadership of Khadafi Janjalani, Abu Sayyaf reoriented its strategy and appears to have gained greater effectiveness as a terrorist organization. Janjalani de-emphasized kidnaping for ransom and instead emphasized developing capabilities for urban bombing. He improved ties with key military factions of the MILF and established cooperation with JI. He also re-emphasized the Islamic nature of Abu Sayyaf. Thus, even though Abu Sayyaf's armed strength fell from an estimated 1,000 in 2002 to 200-400 in 2005, the capabilities of the organization may be growing.[37] Khadafi Janjalani moved some of Abu Sayyaf's operations and leadership to the mainland of western Mindanao. There it reportedly established links with elements of JI, using several MILF base camps where the two groups reportedly engage in joint training with an emphasis on bomb-making carrying urban attacks.[38] Two key JI leaders from Indonesia also relocated to Jolo island in the Sulu island chain southwest of Basilan. In March and April 2003, Abu Sayyaf, JI, and MILF cadre carried out bombings in Davao on Mindanao, which killed 48.

By mid-2005, Jemaah Islamiyah personnel reportedly had trained about 60 Abu Sayyaf members in bomb assembly and detonation.[39] Since March 2004, the Philippine government reportedly has uncovered several Abu Sayyaf plots to carry out attacks in Manila, including the discovery of explosives. One reported target was the United States Embassy. In February 2005, Abu Sayyaf carried out simultaneous bombings in three cities, which indicated a higher level of technical and operational capability. In April 2004, police officials reportedly determined that a February 2004 bombing of a Manila-based ferry, in which 194 people died, was the work of Abu Sayyaf and the Rajah Solaiman Movement, a group of Filipino Muslim converts from the Manila area. According to Philippine national security officials, Abu Sayyaf is training Rajah Solaiman members to carry out terrorist bombings in Manila and several other cities.[40]

U.S. Policy toward Abu Sayyaf

Within a few months after the September 11, 2001 terrorist attack on the United States, the Bush Administration moved to extend direct military support to the Philippines in combating Abu Sayyaf. The U.S. military role appears to be based on three objectives: (1) assist the Philippine military to weaken Abu Sayyaf in its redoubt of Jolo and the other Sulu islands; (2) neutralize Abu Sayyaf-Jemaah Islamiyah training; and (3) kill or capture Abu Sayyaf leaders. The United States committed 1,300 U.S. military personnel in 2002 to support Philippine military operations against Abu Sayyaf on Basilan island. This force completed its mission by the end of 2002. In 2005, the Philippines and the United States developed and implemented a combined operation in western Mindanao against Abu Sayyaf, and U.S. military personnel also participated in noncombat operations on Jolo island in the Sulu island chain.

MNLF and MILF

The U.S. focus on Abu Sayyaf is complicated by the broader Muslim problem in the southern Philippines, including the existence of two separatist movements, the Moro National Liberation Front (MNLF) and the Moro Islamic Liberation Front (MILF). These organizations represent Moro ethnic and religious groups which form a majority of the population in several provinces on Mindanao Island. The MILF was established in 1980 as a splinter group of the more secular MNLF. With an estimated armed strength of 10,000-12,000, the MILF has outgrown its parent organization. Both groups have been in insurrection against the Philippine government for much of the last 30 years. The MNLF signed a peace treaty with Manila in 1996, granting limited autonomy to four Mindanao provinces under an Autonomous Region of Muslim Mindanao (ARMM), while the MILF continued to insist upon the creation of an independent Islamic state.

Peace Agreement and Its Collapse

In August 2008, the Philippine government and the MILF signed a Memorandum of Agreement laying out a framework for a settlement regarding ending MILF insurgency and recognizing their ancestral domain. The Memorandum of Agreement provided for the establishment of a "Bangsamoro Juridical Entity" (BJE), comprised of the ARMM and as many as 737 Muslim majority villages (barangays) outside the ARMM to be determined through plebiscites within 12 months of the signing of the Memorandum. It also laid out the possible future inclusion of 1,459 other "conflict-affected areas." The BJE would have an "associative relationship" with the Philippine government, including "shared authority and responsibility." The Entity would be able to create its own government, election system, banking system, schools, judicial system, and police and internal security forces. The economic resources of the region would be allocated among the Philippine government and the BJE on a 75-25 percent basis favoring the BJE. The Entity could enter into trade and economic relations with foreign countries and would control the resources of waters extending 15 kilometers from its coast.[41]

Immediately after the conclusion of the Memorandum of Agreement, however, Christian politicians on Mindanao filed a suit with the Philippine Supreme Court, calling for the Court to block the Memorandum. The politicians claimed that they had not been consulted about the agreement even though they were the elected officials of areas envisioned for incorporation into the BJE. The Court issued a temporary restraining order on implementation of the Memorandum.

Resistance to the Memorandum reportedly came from not only local Christian leaders and residents, but also entrenched political and economic interests in Mindanao and opposition politicians in Manila. Some critics charged that President Arroyo had schemed to use the Memorandum, which would require changing the government from a unitary form to a federal one, to amend the Philippine constitution, which also would open the way for her to remove the ban on seeking a second term of office.[42] The Supreme Court ruled on October 14, 2008, that the Memorandum was unconstitutional. In an 8-7 decision, the Court held that the "associative relationship" envisaged in the Memorandum was illegal in that it implied eventual independence for the

BJE.[43] Some analysts suggest that the Arroyo Administration's lack of legitimacy and preparation on related constitutional issues and had doomed the Agreement from the start.[44]

Renewed fighting between the AFP and MILF broke out following the collapse of the accord, reportedly resulting in the displacement of over 130,000 villagers and dozens of deaths.[45] Several MILF units attacked Christian villages. The Philippine military launched operations against these "rogue" groups but not the MILF as a whole. In other areas, a cease-fire, first negotiated in 2003, remained in force. However, the truce grew more tenuous when Malaysia withdrew its troops from an International Monitoring Team (IMT) that had been operating in conjunction with the cease-fire. Malaysian personnel had formed the core of the IMT, which was created in 2004 by the Organization of the Islamic Conference (OIC) to help advance the peace process.

Following the Supreme Court ruling of October 14, 2008, the government insisted on new terms for negotiations, including greater consultation with local representatives and organizations. President Arroyo appointed a new chief negotiator in December 2008. The MILF has questioned the government's sincerity in pursuing a settlement and sought a commitment from Manila to adhere to the principles of the Memorandum of Agreement.[46]

Relations between the MILF, JI, and Abu Sayyaf

MILF leaders have denied links with JI and Abu Sayyaf, and reportedly have cooperated with U.S. efforts to hunt Abu Sayyaf leaders. However, there also are many reports linking some local MILF commands with the terrorist organizations. Evidence, including the testimonies of captured Jemaah Islamiyah leaders, has pointed to strong links between certain MILF commanders and JI, including the continued training of JI terrorists in some MILF camps.[47] This training appears to be important to Jemaah Islamiyah's ability to replenish its ranks following arrests of nearly 500 cadre in Indonesia, Malaysia, and Singapore. Furthermore, a stronger collaborative relationship has developed between these MILF commands and Abu Sayyaf since 2002. Zachary Abuza, an expert on Islamic terrorism in Southeast Asia, has identified four of eight MILF base camps as sites of active MILF cooperation with JI and Abu Sayyaf. He also has identified the MILF 's Special Operations Group as facilitating joint training and joint operations with Abu Sayyaf.[48]

There are divisions between civilian and military authorities over strategy toward the MILF. The Arroyo Administration has emphasized negotiation. The AFP has favored a more aggressive strategy and is suspicious of a negotiated settlement. The collaboration between elements of the MILF, JI, and Abu Sayyaf also suggests that key MILF commanders may not support any agreement between the MILF leadership and the Philippine government that does not include outright independence for the Muslim areas of the southern Philippines. In that scenario, the MILF could fracture with hardline elements embracing even more closely JI and Abu Sayyaf, which could give rise to a greater terrorist threat despite a settlement. Furthermore, there is another view that the MILF leadership has a relationship with hard-line MILF commands similar to that between the political organization, Sinn Fein, and the armed wing of the Irish Republican Army. According to this view, the MILF leadership is acting as a front for the hard-line commands, shielding them from the AFP.[49]

Clan Violence

According to some experts, a chief factor contributing to the cycle of violence, corruption, and poverty in Mindanao is clan conflict or vendettas, also known as *rido*. Local police, RP military, and factions of regional separatist organizations have become involved in or exploited such conflicts. In some cases, parties to clan disputes have enlisted state or insurgent military resources; in others, government and rebel forces have recruited local familial groups. *Rido* reportedly also has been a frequent cause of extra-judicial killings in the region.[50]

U.S. Policy toward the MILF

The Bush Administration considered placing the MILF on the U.S. list of terrorist organizations in 2002, and expressed growing concerns over MILF links with JI and JI's use of the Mindanao- Sulawesi (Indonesia) corridor to transport terrorists and weapons.[51] U.S. Administration officials also voiced doubts about the RP government's ability to end Muslim terrorist activity on Mindanao.[52] However, the Arroyo government has opposed characterizing the MILF as terrorist, fearing that such a stance would jeopardize the peace negotiations.[53] Furthermore, some analysts have argued that casting the MILF as terrorist would drive it further into the arms of JI and Abu Sayyaf.[54] The Bush Administration later adopted a policy of supporting the Philippine government-MILF peace negotiations as the best means of de-linking the MILF from JI.[55] This support boosted the Arroyo Administration's position against the AFP's advocacy of a militarily-aggressive strategy. U.S.

Ambassador to the Philippines, Kristie Kenney, signaled Bush Administration support for the 2008 Memorandum of Agreement when she attended the signing of the accord in Kuala Lumpur, Malaysia.[56]

The United States also increased its aid presence in areas of the MILF insurgency. In September 2007, the Bush and Arroyo administrations signed an agreement for a U.S. peace and development program in Mindanao costing $190 million over a five year period. U.S. aid programs in MILF areas involve support for schools, infrastructure programs, and a program to reintegrate ex-MILF fighters into civilian society. Moreover, U.S. military forces in the Philippines have extended civic action programs from Abu Sayyaf conflict areas into MILF regions, and the U.S. military is negotiating with local leaders to expand these programs.[57]

Deepening U.S. involvement has raised the stakes for the United States, especially if the Philippine-MILF conflict worsens in 2009. If the collapse of the August 2008 Memorandum of Agreement should lead to a complete breakdown of negotiations and the cease-fire, the Obama Administration could be confronted with policy decisions regarding the U.S. role in a wider war. The AFP could be expected to propose increased supplies of U.S. arms and military equipment, and likely would argue for a more direct U.S. military role. The Philippine government might change its previous policy of opposition to a U.S. military role and encourage U.S. actions against the MILF similar to those in the joint operations against Abu Sayyaf. If significant elements of the MILF were to move closer to JI and Abu Sayyaf, and if they were able to continue or expand terrorist operations, the Obama Administration could face additional pressures for greater U.S. military involvement.

Given the seemingly intractable nature of the Muslim problem in the southern Philippines, the Obama Administration faces difficult policy choices. One policy dilemma is whether to pressure the Philippine government and political establishment to negotiate an agreement with the MILF along the lines of the 2008 Memorandum of Agreement granting Muslim Mindanao a unique system of autonomy, despite likely opposition to such a settlement among some groups on both sides of the conflict. This scenario appears increasingly plausible, given the perceived poor performance of the Philippine government and political establishment in dealing with and ultimately rejecting the August 2008 accord. A group of former U.S. ambassadors to the Philippines wrote in *The Wall Street Journal Asia* in September 2008 that "the Philippine Supreme Court precipitated a true crisis when it issued a temporary restraining order that aborted" the Memorandum of Agreement and that "something very much like the recently suspended agreement would have to be part of any future settlement."[58] Both RP government and MILF leaders reportedly have called on the United States to get more directly involved in negotiations, but also have expressed suspicion or anger toward some U.S. diplomatic and military activities in Mindanao.[59]

Another, related quandary facing the new Administration is whether to continue current levels of military and development assistance to the RP. Some analysts suggest that although Philippine and joint RP-U.S. military operations have reduced Abu Sayyaf armed strength, a lasting solution in Mindanao requires political will and consensus in Manila that may be beyond the reach of U.S. assistance programs. Furthermore, U.S. aid efforts that aim to address the economic roots of the problem, while they reportedly have garnered goodwill among many local residents, may fail to affect larger trends and stem the tide of violence. Other observers argue that Washington needs to become more engaged and provide greater support, especially non-military assistance, in conflict- ridden areas. Without greater U.S. assistance, they contend, not only would the risk of violence grow, but also U.S. leverage in the Philippines may diminish.[60]

Philippine Communist Party (CPP)

The CPP has directed an insurgency under its New Peoples' Army since the late 1960s. NPA armed strength reached over 25,000 in the early 1980s and was a factor in the downfall of President Ferdinand Marcos in 1986. After Marcos fell and democracy was restored, the NPA declined in strength. However, in recent years, the insurgency has made a slight recovery, reaching an estimated armed force of 8,000 in 2004-2005 and operating in 69 of the Philippines' 79 provinces.[61] Estimated strength in mid-2007 was 7,000.[62] The CPP also has called for attacks on American targets. In August 2002, the Bush Administration placed the CPP and the NPA on the official U.S. list of terrorist organizations. It also pressured the government of the Netherlands to revoke the visa privileges of Communist Party leader, Jose Maria Sison, and other CPP officials who have lived in the Netherlands for a number of years and reportedly direct CPP/NPA operations. In December 2005, the European Union placed the CPP/NPA on its list of terrorist organizations. This could place greater pressure on the Netherlands government to restrict Sison's communist exile group. In June 2007, the Commander of the U.S. Pacific

Command, Admiral Timothy Keating, offered a more direct U.S. support role in AFP operations against the NPA.[63]

FOREIGN RELATIONS

RP-U.S. Security Ties and Military Relations

The Republic of the Philippines is a treaty ally of the United States under the 1951 Mutual Defense Treaty, and relies heavily upon the United States for its external security. Following the terrorist attacks in the United States in September 2001, the RP was designated as a front-line state in the global war on terrorism. The RP has actively supported U.S. counterterrorism efforts in Southeast Asia and has worked with the United States to enhance its own counterterrorism capabilities.[64] The Philippines was designated a Major Non-NATO Ally on October 6, 2003, after President Arroyo announced Manila's support for the U.S.-led invasion of Iraq. This U.S. move was made in part to give the Philippines greater access to American defense equipment and supplies.

In 1991, the Philippine Senate voted 12-11 to revoke the Military Bases Agreement between the RP and the United States, forcing the closure of the Subic Naval base and Clark Air Force base. However, in 1995, President Fidel Ramos invited U.S. forces back on a limited basis, partially in response to China's erection and upgrading of structures on Mischief Reef in the disputed Spratly Islands group. A Visiting Forces Agreement (VFA), allowing joint Philippine-U.S. military operations, was signed by the two countries in 1998 and ratified by the RP Senate in 1999, despite protests by the Catholic Church of the Philippines, leftists, and others. In January 2000, RP-U.S. joint military exercises ("Balikatan" or *Shoulder-to-Shoulder*) were held following a five-year hiatus, in which the United States assumed a non-combat role.

Following the September 11 attacks, Manila offered ports and airports for use by U.S. naval vessels and military aircraft. On March 20, 2003, the Philippines sent a peacekeeping and humanitarian contingent of nearly 100 soldiers and other personnel to Iraq. In July 2004, the Arroyo government withdrew its troops ahead of schedule in exchange for the release of a Filipino truck driver kidnaped by an Iraqi Islamist group. The government reportedly feared that not doing so would provoke a public outcry and raise the risk of kidnaping for hundreds of thousands of other Filipinos working in the region.

Arroyo's action represented an exertion of national over bilateral (U.S.) interests. Officials in the U.S. State Department expressed "disappointment" while some inside and outside of the Administration were angered that Manila "had emboldened the terrorists." President Arroyo's state visit to Beijing in September further added to the apparent chill in RP-U.S. relations. However, the basic ideological and institutional foundations of the RP-U.S. relationship remained strong.[65]

RP-U.S. Operations on Baslian and Jolo Islands

The 2001 terrorist attacks prompted concern over Al Qaeda's links to Abu Sayyaf as well as greater U.S.-Philippine military cooperation. President Arroyo and President Bush agreed on the deployment of U.S. military personnel to the southern Philippines to train and assist the AFP against the Abu Sayyaf group. In February 2002, the United States dispatched 1,300 U.S. troops to provide training, advice, and other non-combat assistance to 1,200 Filipino troops against Abu Sayyaf on the island of Basilan. In consideration of the Filipino Constitution's ban on foreign combat troops operating inside the country, Washington and Manila negotiated special rules of engagement for the Balikatan exercise. U.S. military personnel took direction from Filipino commanders and could use force only to defend themselves. In November 2002, the Arroyo administration signed a Military Logistics and Support Agreement (MLSA), allowing the United States to use the Philippines as a supply base for military operations throughout the region.

The Balikatan exercise reportedly resulted in a significant diminishing of Abu Sayyaf strength on Basilan. Abu Sayyaf's estimated manpower fell to 200-400, but it continued to operate in the Sulu islands south of Basilan and in western Mindanao. In addition, the AFP operations improved as a result of U.S. assistance in intelligence gathering, the supplying of modern equipment, and aid in the planning of operations. The United States and the Philippines negotiated a second phase of U.S. training and support of the AFP, beginning in late 2002, with an objective of training light infantry companies for use against both Muslim insurgents and the NPA.

Continued Abu Sayyaf bombings led the U.S. Defense Department to consider a more extended U.S. assistance program in the southern Philippines, focusing on the Abu Sayyaf concentrations in western Mindanao and on Jolo Island in the Sulu chain. In 2005, the Philippines and the United States developed and implemented combined operations against elements of Abu Sayyaf operating in western Mindanao and Jolo. The operation apparently had three objectives: (1) neutralize Abu Sayyaf-Jemaah Islamiyah training; (2) kill or capture leaders of Abu Sayyaf; and (3) root out the Abu Sayyaf forces and organization on Jolo in a similar fashion as the successful campaign on Basilan in 2002. The U.S. role in western Mindanao reportedly involved intelligence and communications support of the AFP, including the employment of U.S. P-3 surveillance aircraft; deployment of Navy Seal and Special Forces personnel with AFP ground units; and rules restricting U.S. personnel to a non-combat role (although such rules normally would allow U.S. personnel to defend themselves if attacked).[66]

U.S. troops landed on Jolo in 2005. The number of U.S. troops on the island has ranged between 180 and 250. Their mission has been to support 7,000 Filipino troops (ten battalions) on the island against Abu Sayyaf. U.S. military personnel live within Philippine military camps and always operate with AFP units. They can use their weapons only when fired upon.[67] U.S. military support on Jolo has the following main components:

- Training of AFP battalions in conducting operations. This has emphasized training for night combat.
- Providing equipment to the Philippine battalions, including communications equipment and night vision goggles.
- Providing intelligence-gathering technology to the AFP.
- Providing aerial intelligence reconnaissance to locate Abu Sayyaf units and personnel in Jolo's jungles.
- Conducting civic action programs with the AFP aimed at the local populace. U.S. troops have repaired and built piers for fishermen and have constructed roads, water purification installations, and farm markets. They have renovated schools and provided medical care.
- Supporting USAID projects on Jolo and on neighboring Tawi Tawi island, including a new market for Jolo town (the market was destroyed by Abu Sayyaf bombing in 2006) and a major pier on Tawi Tawi.

Reports indicate major successes for the AFP operation on Jolo backed by the United States, but Abu Sayyaf has not been eliminated. Some reports in late 2008 describe limited Abu Sayyaf activity on Basilan.[68] Abu Sayyaf strength on Jolo is down to an estimated 200-300. The group has been pushed back to remote areas on the island. Senior leaders have been killed, including Khadafi Janjalani and Abu Solaiman. However, JI leaders Umar Petek and Dulmatin remain at large on the island. Security has improved in many parts of the island as the AFP has established a permanent presence in many of the areas cleared of Abu Sayyaf. New businesses have emerged in the main towns, and people now venture out at night. The incidence of bombings and ambushes has declined. The attitude of the people of Jolo toward the U.S. military generally has been positive. As on Basilan in 2002, U.S.-conducted and supported civic action projects have been well received.[69]

Another potential U.S. policy decision could come out of the December 2005 agreement among the Philippines, Indonesia, Malaysia, and Brunei for joint maritime patrols in the waters separating them. The agreement specifically covers Mindanao and the Mindanao-Sulawesi corridor. Any future programs to establish maritime interdiction cooperation between the Philippines and its neighbors likely would produce proposals for expanded U.S. military aid and training for the Philippine Navy.

Philippines-China Relations

In the past decade, the Philippines has pursued stable and friendly political and economic relations with China, while relying upon the United States and the Association of Southeast Asian Nations (ASEAN) as security and diplomatic counterweights to the PRC. President Arroyo has made several official visits to China since she assumed the presidency in 2001. Some analysts argue that the People's Republic of China has sought to forestall a greater U.S. military presence in the region, a clash over disputed territory in the Spratlys that might provoke U.S. involvement, and Philippine support of the United States in a possible military crisis involving Taiwan. Rather than take a back seat following the strengthening of Philippine-U.S. ties after 2001, China has offered Manila much-needed military assistance and well as economic aid and investment.[70]

The Philippines' relationship with the PRC has improved markedly since the Mischief Reef Incident in 1995.[71] Faced with pressure from ASEAN, China promised to abide by the United Nations Convention on the Law of the Sea, which states that countries with overlapping claims must resolve them by good faith negotiation. In 2002, Beijing and ASEAN signed the Declaration on the Conduct of Parties in the South China Sea (DOC), which many in the region hope will evolve into a formal code of conduct that promotes a peaceful resolution of territorial disputes. In 2003, China acceded to the Treaty of Amity and Cooperation in Southeast Asia, which renounces the use of force and calls for greater economic and political cooperation.

Some analysts contend that the Arroyo government's withdrawal of RP military personnel from Iraq in July 2004 created a temporary chill in Manila's relations with Washington, while Philippine contacts with Beijing became warmer. President Arroyo paid an official visit to China in September 2004. In November 2004, RP and PRC military officials signed a Memorandum of Understanding on Defense Cooperation, and in May 2005, the two countries signed agreements related to the following: annual defense and security dialogues; PRC training of AFP soldiers; Chinese technical assistance to the AFP; and a gift of non-lethal military equipment worth $6 million.[72]

Some argue that China has exploited what many Southeast Asians perceive as a one-dimensional U.S. view of the region, with its focus on counterterrorism, by emphasizing their development needs. In the past few years, China has become one of the RP's biggest trading partners, a major investor in infrastructure, energy, agriculture, and mining, and a significant provider of foreign aid, mostly in the form of concessional loans which rival those of Japan, the Asian Development Bank, and the World Bank. The Philippines is now the largest recipient of PRC loans in Southeast Asia, which reportedly total $2 billion in pledged financing, of which about half has been disbursed.[73] One of the largest PRC-funded projects in the country is the $1 billion North Rail line on Luzon.[74]

China's beneficence has also been a source of scandals roiling Philippine politics. In 2007, the RP government signed a $329 million contract with ZTE Corporation of China to build a national broadband network linking government units. The Commissions of Elections chairman, Benjamin Abalos, was later accused of bribing Philippine and Chinese officials and a rival Philippine telecom company in exchange for their support of the ZTE deal. Abalos resigned from his position in October 2007 while President Arroyo canceled the project. ZTE denied involvement in any corrupt activities.[75]

Some Philippine lawmakers have accused the Arroyo government of compromising the country's sovereignty and foreign relations in exchange for PRC loans and other forms of cooperation. The Joint Marine Seismic Undertaking (JMSU), a three-year agreement signed in 2004 and 2005 by the China National Offshore Oil Corp., the Philippine National Oil Corp., and PetroVietnam, involved seismic data gathering in the Spratly Islands area in preparation for oil exploration activities. Some Philippine lawmakers protested that the JMSU covered not only disputed territory but also undisputed Philippine islands as well as one island claimed and occupied by Taiwan.[76] Furthermore, other critics argued that the agreement undermined ASEAN efforts to deal with China as a bloc. The RP government did not renew the JMSU in 2008 due to opposition in the legislature.

Although some Philippine politicians and opinion leaders have been critical of RP-China economic arrangements, some analysts argue that the focus of their disapproval has been their domestic political opponents rather than the PRC. Meanwhile, many Filipinos view RP-China relations as positive overall and China's intentions as benign. They have expressed more concern about political corruption and the lack of government transparency regarding these deals than about China per se. In September 2008, President Arroyo created a special government panel to oversee projects funded by PRC aid money, a move expected to be popular with the public.[77]

FILIPINO VETERANS

Many Filipino veterans of World War II, who fought with the U.S. Armed Forces against the Japanese military, claimed that the United States government promised them U.S. citizenship and full veterans' benefits. However, following the war, congressional legislation granted full veterans benefits only to Regular ("Old") Philippine Scouts, while limiting eligibility among three groups—the "New" Philippine Scouts, Recognized Guerrilla Forces, and Commonwealth Army of the Philippines. The U.S. Congress expanded benefits to these three groups over the years. In December 2003, the Bush Administration signed a measure that extended Veterans Affairs health benefits to all Filipino veterans living in the United States. Filipino veterans organizations continued to push for legislation that would provide more complete benefits, including health care to veterans living in the Philippines. In 2008, fewer than 18,000 of over 200,000 Filipino WWII veterans reportedly were still alive, including 6,000 residing in the United States, according to some estimates.[78]

Two measures were introduced in the 110th Congress, H.R. 760 and S. 57, that would grant full veterans benefits to the New Philippine Scouts, Recognized Guerrilla Forces, and Commonwealth Army of the Philippines, similar to those received by U.S. veterans and "Old" Philippine Scouts.[79] The Veterans Benefits Enhancement Act of 2007 (S. 1315), as passed by the Senate, incorporated elements of S. 57, while the House version of the bill did not contain such provisions.[80] In addition, the Filipino Veterans Equity Act of 2008 (H.R. 6897, introduced on September 15, 2008) would establish the

Filipino Veterans Equity Compensation Fund through which one-time payments would be made ($15,000 for U.S. citizens and $9,000 for non-U.S. citizens) to certain eligible persons who served in the New Philippine Scouts, Recognized Guerrilla Forces, and Commonwealth Army of the Philippines. The Filipino Veterans Assistance Act of 2008 (H.R. 6645), introduced on July 29, 2008, would authorize the President to provide assistance to the Republic of the Philippines for the purpose of aiding these Filipino veterans.

S. 68, introduced by Senator Inouye on January 6, 2009 (11 1th Congress), would require the Secretary of the Army to determine the validity of the claims of certain Filipinos that they performed military service on behalf of the United States during World War II. Such certification would qualify such persons or their survivors to receive any military, veterans', or other benefits under U.S. laws.

TIME LINE: MAJOR HISTORICAL EVENTS

1542:	Spaniards claim the islands and name them the Philippines.
1890s:	Insurgency against Spanish rule
1898:	Spanish-American War—Spain cedes the Philippines to the United States
1899:	Insurgency against U.S. rule
1935:	Plebiscite approves establishment of Commonwealth of Philippines; Country is promised full independence in ten years
1941:	Japan invades
1944:	U.S. forces retake islands
1946:	Philippines granted full independence
1965:	Ferdinand Marcos becomes president
1969:	Muslim separatists begin guerrilla war
1972:	Marcos declares Marshall Law
1983:	Opposition leader Benigno Aquino assassinated
1986:	Corazon Aquino assumes presidency following "People Power" protests
1989:	Coup attempt suppressed
1992:	Aquino's defense minister, Fidel Ramos, wins presidency. United States closes Subic Bay Naval

	Station
1996:	Philippines government reaches truce with Moro National Liberation Front (MNLF)
1998:	Film star Joseph Estrada elected President
2000:	Impeachment proceedings begin against Estrada on allegations of corruption and violation of the constitution
2001(January):	Amid mass street protests, Estrada's vice-President, Gloria Macapagal-Arroyo, is sworn in as President. Estrada is arrested for plundering state funds
2001 (March):	Moro Islamic Liberation Front (MILF) declares cease fire
2002:	Philippines and United States hold joint military exercises
2002:	Terrorist bombs detonate in Manila and Zamboanga city, killing ten persons
2003 (July):	RP government signs cease fire with MILF
2003 (July):	RP soldiers (AFP) seize shopping center in mutiny
2004:	Peace talks between government and NPA start but are later called off
2004 (June):	Macapagal-Arroyo wins Presidential election
2004 (July):	Philippines withdraws peacekeeping troops from Iraq
2005:	Heavy fighting between AFP and MILF breaks cease fire
2005:	President Arroyo comes under pressure to resign over allegations of vote-rigging
2006:	President Arroyo declares week-long state of emergency following alleged discovery of coup plot.
2007:	In mid-term congressional elections, pro-Arroyo parties gain strength in the House but lose seats in the Senate.
2008 (August):	Peace agreement between the government and MILF collapses after Supreme Court issues a temporary stay.

Figure 1. Map of The Philippines

End Notes

[1] Catharin Dalpino, "Separatism and Terrorism in the Philippines: Distinctions and Options for U.S. Policy," *Testimony before the Subcommittee on East Asia and the Pacific, House International Relations Committee*, June 10, 2003.

[2] Asian Nation http://www.asian-nation; Migration Policy Institute (September 2008) http://migrationinformation.org/; Department of State, "Background Note: Philippines," October 2008.

[3] Herman Joseph S. Kraft, "The Philippine-U.S. Alliance: A Strategic Partnership in Tactical Mode," Center for Strategic and International Studies, *Southeast Asia Bulletin* (October 2008).

[4] *Global Trade Atlas*.

[5] The basis of the accusation was a recorded telephone conversation of Arroyo with a member of the Commission of Elections prior to the voting. According to reports, in the call, she told the commissioner that she wanted to secure a "one million vote margin," and he expressed support for her wish. In June 2005, President Macapagal-Arroyo publicly apologized for a "lapse in judgment" but vowed to remain in office. Paul Alexander, "Support for Philippine President Crumbles," *Washington Post*, July 8, 2005.

[6] "Philippine President Arroyo Looking Better in Poll," Gulfnews.com, October 14, 2008.

[7] Alexis Douglas B. Romero, "DeCastro Still Top Pick but Villar Narrows Gap (2010 Elections)," *Business World*, November 7, 2008.

[8] Mely Caballero-Anthony, "U.S.-Philippine Relations after the Iraq Crisis," *PacNet No. 35*, August 19, 2004.

[9] Joel D. Adriano, "Arroyo's Risky Politics of Patronage," *Asia Times Online*, December 9, 2008.

[10] Freedom in the World Survey http://www.freedomhouse.org.

[11] Economist Intelligence Unit, *Country Profile 2008 (Philippines)*.

[12] Alex Magno, "The Perils of Pedestals," *Time Asia*, July 11, 2005.

[13] Carlos H. Conde, "Deaths and Fraud Reports Mar Philippine Vote," *New York Times*, May 15, 2007.

[14] Bruce Gale, "Arroyo in for Reform Headache," *The Straits Times*, July 4, 2007.

[15] "Filipino Reporter Shot; Official Condemns Attack," *International Herald Tribune*, August 5, 2008.

[16] Alan Sipress, "A 'Culture of Impunity' Protects Journalists' Killers in Philippines," *Washington Post*, September 12, 2004. "Gunmen Kill Radio Commentator in South Philippines," *Reuters News*, July 18, 2006.

[17] Simon Montlake, "In Capitalist Asia, Philippines Still Grapples with Communists," *Christian Science Monitor*, December 7, 2005.

[18] "Philippine Police Reject 635 Cases on Rights Group's Extrajudicial Killings List," *BBC Monitoring Asia Pacific*, February 4, 2008.

[19] "The Dirty War that Deepens Philippine Divisions," *International Herald Tribune*, August 22, 2006; Donald Kirk, "Filipinos Protest Steady Rise of Political Killings," *Christian Science Monitor*, May 31, 2006.

[20] "Rights Activists Uncowed as Blood Letting in Philippines Continues," *Agence France-Presse*, November 12, 2006.

[21] "Another Journalist Shot Dead," *Philippine Daily Inquirer*, February 20, 2007; Press Statement: Professor Philip Alston, Special Rapporteur of the United Nations Human Rights Council on Extrajudicial, Summary or Arbitrary Executions, Manila, February 21, 2007.

[22] U.S. Department of State, Country Reports on Human Rights Practices—2007, March 11, 2008 (Philippines).

[23] Katherine Adraneda, "RP Report Card on HR: Abysmal," *The Philippine Star*, January 3, 2009.

[24] Measured in "purchasing power parity" (PPP) terms, which factors in cost of living.

[25] Central Intelligence Agency, *World Factbook;* United Nations Development Programme. The HDI ranks countries according to human development indicators of life expectancy, education, literacy, and gross domestic product.

[26] Sarah Efron, "Calling out Bangalore; Rivalling India, the Philippines See Prosperity in Offshore Outsourcing," *National Post*, September 6, 2008.

[27] Economist Intelligence Unit, *Country Report—Philippines*, January 2009.

[28] "RP is 4th in Worldwide Remittances," *The Manila Times*, March 25, 2008.

[29] *Global Trade Atlas.*

[30] Maila Ager, "RP, US Sign Agriculture Cooperation Pact," Inquirer.net, June 25, 2008.

[31] PCCI Upbeat on Prospects for RP-US Trade Agreement," *Business World*, July 30, 2008.

[32] For further information, see U.S. Department of State, *Congressional Budget Justification for Foreign Operations, FY2009*; CRS Report RL3 1362, *U.S. Foreign Aid to East and South Asia: Selected Recipients*, by Thomas Lum.

[33] See CRS Report RL31672, *Terrorism in Southeast Asia*, by Bruce Vaughn et al..

[34] "Philippine Forces Capture Abu Sayyaf Militant Suspected of Beheading Marines,"*International Herald Tribune*, January 21, 2008.

[35] Abuza, Zachary. *Balik-Terrorism: The Return of the Abu Sayyaf Group.* Carlisle, U.S. Army War College, 2005.

[36] The ASG reportedly provided support to Ramzi Yousef, an Al Qaeda agent convicted of planning the 1993 bombing of the World Trade Center. In 1994, Yousef rented an apartment in Manila where he made plans and explosives in an attempt to blow up 11 U.S. passenger jets simultaneously over the Pacific Ocean.

[37] Abuza, *Balik-Terrorism*, op. cit., p. 27. Mogato, Manny. "Fighting in the Philippine South Rages, Soldier Killed." *Reuters News*, November 24, 2005.

[38] Ibid., pp. 14-19, 22-24.

[39] Mogato, Manny. "Philippine Rebels Linking up with Foreign Jihadists." *Reuters*, August 21, 2005. Del Puerto, Luige A. "PNP [Philippine National Police]: Alliance of JI, RP Terrorists Strong." *Philippine Daily Inquirer* (internet version), November 20, 2005.

[40] Abuza, *Balik-Terrorism*, op. cit., p. 36.

[41] *International Crisis Group*, "The Philippines: The Collapse of Peace in Mindanao." October 23, 2008, p. 3-6. Fe Zamora, "Bangsomoro to Get Own State: Government, MILF to Sign Ancestral Domain Pact Tuesday," *Philippine Daily Inquirer* (internet), August 3, 2008.

[42] Brett M. Decker, "Gloria's Terror Gambit," *Wall Street Journal Asia*, August 7, 2008, p. 12.

[43] International Crisis Group," The Philippines: the Collapse of Peace in Mindanao." October 23, 2008, p. 11-12.

[44] Carl Baker, "Looking Forward in Mindanao," *PacNet #45*, September 4, 2008.

[45] Jim Gomez, "Philippine Troops Press Assault on Muslim Rebels," *Washington Post*, August 11, 2008.

[46] Simon Roughneen, "Philippine Unease," *Washington Times*, October 30, 2008, p. B1. Alexis B. Romero and Darwin T. Wee, "New Peace Panel Head a Sign to Restart Stalled Negotiations," *Business World Online*, December 2, 2008. ETM, "Longer Christmas Truce Recommended," *Business World Online*, December 16, 2008.

[47] Isagani P. Palma, "Military Links MILF to Jemaah Islamiyah," *Manila Times Online*, November 30, 2008.

[48] Interview with Zachary Abuza, January 3, 2006.

[49] Commentary on ABC Radio News, December 28, 2005.

[50] Wilfredo Magno Torres III, ed. *Rido: Clan Feuding and Conflict Management in Mindanao*, The Asia Foundation, 2007; "Extrajudicial Killings in the Philippines: Strategies to End the Violence," Statement by G. Eugene Martin, U.S. Institute of Peace, Hearing before the Senate Foreign Relations Subcommittee on East Asian and Pacific Affairs, March 14, 2007; "'Rido' Worsens Conflict in South, Says Study," Inquirer.net, October 29, 2007.

[51] Abuza, *Balik-Terrorism*, op. cit., p. 42.

[52] In April 2005, U.S. Embassy Charge d'Affairs in Manila, Joseph Mussomeli, caused an uproar among RP officials when he stated that parts of Muslim Mindanao, with its poverty, lawlessness, porous borders, and links to regional terrorist groups, could develop into an "Afghanistan-style" situation. In May 2005, U.S. Ambassador to the Philippines, Francis Ricciardone, referred to Cotabato province in southern Mindanao as a "doormat" for Muslim terrorists. Jacinto, Al, "War on Corruption, Poverty in South Must be Won First," *Manila Times (Internet Edition)*, September 11, 2007.

[53] Gloria's powers of persuasion. *Far Eastern Economic Review*, December 12, 2002. p. 10.

[54] "Mindanao Impasse: Prospects for Peace and What it Means for America," Heritage Foundation, October 24, 2008.

[55] *Asia Security Monitor* No. 147, November 30, 2005. "U.S. Says Peace Deal in Manila May Pressure JI." Reuters News, October 22, 2005.

[56] "Mess in Mindanao," *Wall Street Journal Asia*, August 22, 2008, p. 14.

[57] Patricio N. Abinales, "And What of America?" *Manila Times*, August 29, 2008. "U.S. Military Projects Up in Lanao Del Norte," *Mindanao Examiner Online*, November 25, 2008.

[58] Stephen Bosworth, et. al., "Fixing Mindanao," *Wall Street Journal Asia*, September 30, 2008, p. 16.

[59] Julmunir I. Jannaral, "MILF Says US Government Has Unfinished Obligation Toward Moro People," Manila Times Online, December 1, 2008. Fabio Scarpello, "U.S. Diplomat Meets Philippines Rebels amid Ongoing Controversy over U.S. Presence," *World Politics Review* (internet), February 28, 2008.

[60] "Mindanao Impasse," op. cit.

[61] Hepinstall, Sonya and O'Callaghan, John. "Interview—Communists Pose Biggest Threat to Philippines." *Reuters News*, January 10, 2006.

[62] Labog-Javellana, Juliet and Mallari, Delfin T. "AFP: We Can Beat NPA Rebels Without US Help." *Makati City* Inquirer.net, June 29, 2007.

[63] Ibid.

[64] U.S. Department of State, *FY2009 Congressional Budget Justification.*

[65] Mely Caballero-Anthony, "U.S.-Philippine Relations after the Iraq Crisis," *PacNet No. 35*, August 19, 2004; Andrea Koppel, "U.S. Confused by Philippine Decision," CNN, July 13, 2004; Peter Brookes, "Saying 'Yes' to Terror," *The Heritage Foundation*, July 16, 2004.

[66] Bonner, Raymond and Conde, Carlos H. "U.S. and Philippines Join Forces to Pursue Terrorist Leader." *New York Times*, July 23, 2005.

[67] Hookway, James. "Terror Fight Scores in the Philippines." *The Wall Street Journal Asia*, June 20, 2007. p. A.

[68] Darwin T. Wee, Alexis B. Romero and Carmelito Q. Francisco, "Pursuit of Bandits Ordered Intensified," *Business World Online*, December 15, 2008.

[69] Ibid. Montlake, Simon. "US Troops in Philippines Defy Old Stereotype." *Christian Science Monitor*, March 1, 2007. p. 7.

[70] Renato Cruz De Castro, "China, the Philippines, and U.S. Influence in Asia," *Asian Outlook (AEI Online)*, July 6, 2007.

[71] Carl Baker, "China-Philippines Relations: Cautious Cooperation," *Asia-Pacific Center for Security Studies*, October 2004.

[72] Ian Story, "China and the Philippines: Moving Beyond the South China Sea Dispute," *China Brief*, The Jamestown Foundation, October 25, 2006.

[73] Katrice R. Jalbuena, "Ties with PRC, Now Most Important to RP, Also Involves Security Matters," *Manila Times*, June 29, 2008; New York University Wagner School, "Understanding Chinese Foreign Aid: A Look at China's Development Assistance to Africa, Southeast Asia, and Latin America," report prepared for the Congressional Research Service, April 25, 2008.

[74] Walter Lohman, "Off the Rails in the Philippines," Heritage Foundation, *WebMemo no. 1856*, March 14, 2008; Darwin G. Amojelar, "Chinese Loans to RP Rising," *The Manila Times*, December 3, 2007.

[75] Allen Kicken, "The Philippines in 2007," *Asian Survey*, Vol. XLVIII, No. 1 (January/February 2008).

[76] The Philippines and China signed the agreement in 2004; Vietnam signed on in 2005. The Spratlys are claimed in whole or in part by the Philippines, China, Vietnam, Malaysia, Taiwan, and Brunei. Barry Wain, "Manila's Bungle in the South China Sea," *Far Eastern Economic Review*, Jan/Feb 2008; "Sold: 24,000 Sq. Km.," *Malaya News*, March 8, 2008; "Philippines: Energy Chief Says Joint Exploration Pact with China, Vietnam, Lapses," *BBC Monitoring Asia Pacific*, July 12, 2008.

[77] "Macapagal Sets up Oversight of China Projects," *Financial Times*, September 26, 2008.

[78] Jennie L. Ilustre, "WW2 Filvets Oppose Lump Sum US Pension Bill," *Malaya*, September 25, 2008.

[79] See CRS Report RL33 876, *Overview of Filipino Veterans' Benefits*, by Sidath Viranga Panangala, Carol D. Davis, and Christine Scott.

[80] S.Rept. 110-148, Title IV.

In: Republic of the Philippines and U.S. Relations ISBN: 978-1-61668-951-3
Editor: Margaret R. Voigt

Chapter 2

OVERVIEW OF FILIPINO VETERAN'S BENEFITS*

Christine Scott, Sidath Viranga Panangala and Carol D. Davis

SUMMARY

The United States has had a continuous relationship with the Philippine Islands since 1898, when they were acquired by the United States as a result of the Spanish-American War. Filipinos have served in, and with, the U.S. Armed Forces since the Spanish-American War, and especially during World War II. The Islands remained a possession of the United States until 1946.

Since 1946, Congress has passed several laws affecting various categories of Filipino veterans. Many of these laws have been liberalizing laws that have provided Filipino World War II veterans with medical and monetary benefits similar to benefits available to U.S. veterans.

However, not all veterans' benefits are available to veterans of the Commonwealth Army of the Philippines, Recognized Guerrilla Forces, and New Philippine Scouts. In the 110th Congress, two measures, H.R. 760 and S. 57, have been introduced that would eliminate the distinction between the

* This is an edited, reformatted and augmented version of a CRS Report for Congress publication dated February 2009.

Regular, or "Old," Philippine Scouts and the other three groups of veterans—the Commonwealth Army of the Philippines, Recognized Guerrilla Forces, and New Philippine Scouts—making them all fully eligible for veterans' benefits similar to those received by U.S. veterans.

This chapter defines the four specific groups (Regular Philippine Scouts, Commonwealth Army of the Philippines, Recognized Guerilla Forces, and New Philippine Scouts) of Filipino nationals who served under the command of the United States, outlines the Rescission Acts of 1946, benefit changes since 1946, current benefits for Filipino veterans by group, and recent legislative proposals and legislation, including the American Recovery and Reinvestment Act of 2009 (ARRA, P.L. 111-5).

BACKGROUND

The Philippine Islands became a U.S. possession in 1898, when they were ceded from Spain following the Spanish-American War (1898-1902).[1] In 1934, Congress passed the Philippine Independence Act (Tydings-McDuffie Act, P.L. 73-127), which set a 10-year timetable for the eventual independence of the Philippines and in the interim established a Commonwealth of the Philippines vested with certain powers over its internal affairs. In 1935, the Philippine Constitution was adopted and the first President of the Philippines was elected. The granting of full independence was ultimately delayed until 1946 because of the Japanese occupation of the Islands from 1942-1945.

Among other things, P.L. 73-127 reserved to the United States the power to maintain military bases and armed forces in the Philippines and, upon order of the President of the United States, the right to call into the service of the U.S. Armed Forces all military forces organized by the Philippine government. On July 26, 1941, President Franklin D. Roosevelt issued an executive order inducting all military forces of the Commonwealth of the Philippines under the command of a newly created command structure called the United States Armed Forces of the Far East (USAFFE). These units remained under USAFFE command through the duration of World War II (WWII), until authority over them was returned to the Commonwealth at the time of independence.

From time to time since 1946, Congress has passed laws providing, and in some instances repealing, benefits to Filipino veterans. This chapter provides an overview of major Filipino veterans legislation enacted by Congress since

1946. The report begins by defining the specific groups of Filipino nationals who served under the command of the United States, outlines the Rescission Acts of 1946, the changes to benefits for Filipino veterans since 1946, and recent legislative proposals.

Table 1, at the end of this chapter, shows the current benefits for Filipino veterans and survivors.

Regular, or "Old," Philippine Scouts

These were soldiers who enlisted as Philippine Scouts prior to October 6, 1945. They were members of a small, regular component of the U.S. Army that was considered to be in regular active service. The Regular Philippine Scouts were part of the U.S. Army throughout their existence, and are entitled to all benefits administered by the Department of Veterans Affairs (VA) by the same criteria that apply to any veteran of U.S. military service.[2]

Commonwealth Army of the Philippines

These soldiers enlisted in the organized military forces of the Government of the Philippines under the provisions of the Philippine Independence Act of 1934. They served before July 1, 1946, while such forces were in the service of the U.S. Armed Forces pursuant to the military order of the President of the United States dated July 26, 1941.

Recognized Guerrilla Forces

These were individuals who served in resistance units recognized by, and cooperating with, the U.S. Armed Forces during the period April 20, 1942, to June 20, 1946.[3] They served primarily during the Japanese occupation of the Islands. Following reoccupation of the Islands by the U.S. Armed Forces, they became a recognized part of the Commonwealth Army of the Philippines by order of the President of the Philippines.

New Philippine Scouts

These were Philippine citizens who served with the U.S. Armed Forces with the consent of the Philippine government between October 6, 1945, and June 30, 1947, and who were discharged from such service under conditions other than dishonorable.[4] Since these scouts were recruited as a result of the Armed Forces Voluntary Recruitment Act of 1945 (P.L. 79-190), they are referred to as “New” Scouts.

RESCISSION ACTS OF 1946

In 1946, Congress passed the first Supplemental Surplus Appropriation Rescission Act (P.L. 79-301) and the second Supplemental Surplus Appropriation Rescission Act (P.L. 79-391), which came to be commonly known as the “Rescission Acts of 1946.” It should be noted that the Rescission Acts of 1946 applied only to Filipino veterans who were members of the Commonwealth Army of the Philippines, Recognized Guerrilla Forces, or the New Philippine Scouts. Veterans who served as Regular, or “Old,” Philippine Scouts were categorized as U.S. veterans. They were, and remain, generally entitled to all veterans’ benefits for which any other U.S. veteran is eligible.

First Supplemental Surplus Appropriation Rescission Act (P.L. 79- 301)

Enacted on February 18, 1946, P.L. 79-301 authorized a $200 million appropriation to the Commonwealth Army of the Philippines with a provision limiting benefits for these veterans to: (1) compensation for service-connected disabilities[5] or death; and (2) National Service Life Insurance contracts already in force.[6] Furthermore, this provision included bill language stating that

> Service before July 1, 1946, in the organized military forces of the government of the Commonwealth of the Philippines while such forces were in the service of the Armed Forces of the United States pursuant to the military order of the President, dated July 26, 1941 ... shall not be deemed to have been active military, naval or air service for the purposes of any law of the United States conferring rights, privileges, or benefits upon any person by

reason of the service of such person or the service of any other person in the Armed Forces.[7]

Because of differences between economic conditions and living standards in the United States and the Philippines, P.L. 79-301 also provided that any benefits paid to Commonwealth Army veterans would be paid at the rate of one Philippine peso to each dollar[8] for a veteran who was a member of the U.S. Armed Forces, with the assumption that one peso would obtain for Philippine veterans in the Philippine economy the equivalent of $1 of goods and services for American veterans in the American economy. Prior to the enactment of P.L. 79-301, Commonwealth Army veterans were determined by the then Veterans' Administration to be eligible for U.S. veterans' benefits.[9]

Second Supplemental Surplus Appropriation Rescission Act (P.L. 79-391)

Enacted on May 27, 1946, P.L. 79-391 provided that service in the Philippine Scouts (the New Philippine Scouts) under Section 14 of the Armed Forces Voluntary Recruitment Act of 1945 (P.L. 79-190) shall not be deemed to have been active military or air service for the purpose of any laws administered by the Veterans' Administration.

Legislative Intent of the Rescission Acts

There is little background information on the intent of Congress in passing the first Rescission Act, as it affects veterans of the Commonwealth Army. However, statements made by Senator Carl Hayden during hearings on the second Rescission Act, which affected New Philippine Scouts, provide some indication of legislative intent in the passage of the first Rescission Act, and to the subsequent passage of the second Rescission Act. Furthermore, other events at the time may provide some context in which the Rescission Acts were considered.

At the end of World War II, when Congress was considering a $200 million appropriation for the support of the Philippine Army, Senator Carl Hayden of the Senate Committee on Appropriations sent a letter to General Omar Bradley, then Director of the Veterans' Administration, requesting information concerning the status of the Filipino servicemen and the potential cost of their veterans benefits. In his response to the committee, General Bradley indicated that the total cost of paying veterans' benefits to members of the Philippine Commonwealth Army and their dependents, under then existing veterans' laws, would amount in the long run (75 years) to about $3 billion. It seems clear from Senator Hayden's statements that the passage of the first Rescission Act was meant to balance competing financial interests by providing some benefits, such as pensions for service-connected disability or death, while at the same time reducing the U.S. liability for future benefits. To accomplish this, Senator Hayden, Senator Russell and Senator Brooks included language by way of an amendment to the first Rescission bill stating that service by members of the Commonwealth Army was not considered active military, naval, or air service in the U.S. Armed Forces. Furthermore, hearings on the second Rescission Act also clearly indicate that it was Congress's intent to limit wartime benefits given to New Philippine Scouts:

> Because neither the President nor the Congress has declared an end to the war, a [New] Philippine Scout upon separation from service would be entitled to the same benefits as an American soldier who served in time of war. Unless this amendment [to the second Rescission Act] is adopted, a [New Philippine] Scout would be entitled to claim every advantage provided for the G.I. bill of rights such as loans, education, unemployment compensation, hospitalization, domiciliary care and other benefits provided by the laws administered by the Veterans' Administration. Because hostilities have actually ceased, the amendment makes it perfectly clear that these wartime benefits do not apply and that the 50,000 men now authorized to be enlisted in the [New] Philippine Scouts will be entitled only to pensions resulting from service-connected disability or service-connected death.[10]

In addition, the passage of the Rescission Acts may have been influenced by other bills under consideration by Congress at that time. In 1946, Congress passed the Philippine Rehabilitation Act (P.L. 79-3 70) and the Philippine Trade Act (P.L. 79-371). The terms of the Rehabilitation Act required the United States to pay claims for rehabilitation of the Philippines and war damage claims up to $620 million. Of this sum, $220 million was allocated for repair of public property. The remaining $400 million was allocated for war damage claims of individuals and associations. The Philippine Trade Act provided for free trade between the United States and the Philippines until July 3, 1954. These bills under consideration at the time would have provided economic stability to the newly emerging nation. According to Senator Hayden:

> As I see it, the best thing the American government can do is to help the Filipino people to help themselves. Where there was a choice between expenditures for the rehabilitation of the economy of the Philippine Islands and payments in cash to Filipino veterans, I am sure it is better to spend any equal sum of money, for example, on improving the roads and port facilities. What the Filipino veteran needs is steady employment rather than to depend for his living upon a monthly payment sent from the United States.[11]

Therefore, it seems clear that Congress considered the Rescission Acts in the context of providing for the comprehensive economic development of the soon to be sovereign Republic of the Philippines.

BENEFIT CHANGES, 1946-1998

Health Care Benefits

P.L. 80-865

Enacted on July 1, 1948, P.L. 80-865 authorized aid not to exceed $22.5 million for the construction and equipping of a hospital in the Philippines to provide care for Commonwealth Army veterans and Recognized Guerrilla Forces. P.L. 80-865 also authorized $3.3 million annually for a five-year grant program to reimburse the Republic of the Philippines for the care and treatment of service-connected conditions of those veterans. In 1951, plans for a new hospital were completed, and construction of a new hospital began in 1953. Work was completed at a total cost of $9.4 million, and the hospital was dedicated on November 20, 1955.[12] This facility came to be known as the Veterans Memorial Medical Center (VMMC), and the facility was turned over to the Philippine government. The hospital is now organized under the Philippine Department of National Defense.[13]

P.L. 82-311

Enacted on April 9, 1952, P.L. 82-311 authorized the President to transfer the United States Army Provisional Philippine Scout Hospital at Fort McKinley, Philippines, including all the equipment contained in the hospital, to the Republic of the Philippines. P.L. 82-311 also authorized a five- year grant program to reimburse the Republic of the Philippines for the medical care of Regular Philippine Scouts undergoing treatment at the United States Army Provisional Philippine Scout Hospital.

P.L. 83-421

Enacted on June 18, 1954, P.L. 83-421 extended the five-year grant program for an additional five years, through June 30, 1958, and authorized payments of $3 million for the first year, and then payments decreasing by $500,000 each year. No change was made to the provision stating that funds could be used for either medical care on a contract basis or for hospital operations.

P.L. 85-461

The VMMC was originally intended to provide care for service-connected conditions only. However, P.L. 85-461 enacted on June 18, 1958, expanded its use to include veterans of any war for any nonservice-connected disability if such veterans were unable to defray the expenses of necessary hospital care. The VA was authorized to pay for such care on a contract basis. P.L. 85- 461 also authorized the President, with the concurrence of the Republic of the Philippines, to modify the agreement between the United States and the Philippines with respect to hospital and medical care for Commonwealth Army veterans, and Recognized Guerrilla Forces.[14] The law stated that in lieu of any grants made after July 1, 1958, the VA may enter into a contract with the VMMC under which the United States would pay for hospital care in the Republic of the Philippines for Commonwealth Army veterans and Recognized Guerrilla Forces determined by the VA to need such hospital care for service-connected disabilities. P.L. 85-461 also required that the contract must be entered into before July 1, 1958, would be for a period of not more than five consecutive fiscal years beginning July 1, 1958, and shall provide for payments for such hospital care at a per diem rate to be jointly determined for each fiscal year by the two governments to be fair and reasonable.

P.L. 85-461 also authorized the Republic of the Philippines to use at their discretion beds, equipment, and other facilities of the VMMC at Manila, not required for hospital care of Commonwealth Army veterans with service-connected disabilities, for the care of other persons.[15]

P.L. 88-40

Enacted on June 13, 1963, P.L. 88-40 extended the grant program for another five years, through June 30, 1968. Under provisions of P.L. 88-40, costs for any one fiscal year were not to exceed $500,000.

P.L. 89-612

Enacted on September 30, 1966, P.L. 89-612 expanded the grant program to include hospital care at the VMMC for Commonwealth Army veterans, determined by the VA to need such care for nonservice-connected disabilities if they were unable to defray the expenses of such care. P.L. 89- 612 also authorized the provision of hospital care to New Philippine Scouts for service-connected disabilities, and for nonservice-connected conditions if they were enlisted before July 4, 1946, the date of Philippine independence. P.L. 89-612 also authorized $500,000 for replacing and upgrading equipment and for restoring the physical plant of the hospital. P.L. 89-612 also provided an annual appropriation of $100,000 for six years, beginning in 1967, for grants to the VMMC for medical research and training of health service personnel.

Veterans Health Care Expansion Act of 1973 (P.L. 93-82)

Enacted on August 1, 1973, P.L. 93-82 authorized nursing home care for eligible Commonwealth Army veterans and New Philippine Scouts. P.L. 93-82 also provided that available beds, equipment, and other facilities at the VMMC could be made available, at the discretion of the Republic of the Philippines, for other persons, subject to: (1) priority of admissions and hospitalizations given to Commonwealth Army veterans or New Philippine scouts needing hospital care for service-connected conditions; and (2) the use of available facilities on a contract basis for hospital care or medical services for persons eligible to receive care from the VA. P.L. 93-82 also authorized funding of up to $2 million annually for medical care, and provided for annual grants of up to $50,000 for education and training of health service personnel at the VMMC, and of up to $50,000 for replacing and upgrading equipment and maintaining the physical plant.

Veterans' Health Care, Training, and Small Business Loan Act of 1981 (P.L. 97-72)

Enacted on November 3, 1981, P.L. 97-72 made substantial changes to then existing law. P.L. 97- 72 amended section 632 [now 1732] of Title 38 "to make it explicitly clear that it is the position of the United States that the primary responsibility for providing medical care and treatment for Commonwealth Army veterans and New Philippine Scouts rests with the Republic of the Philippines."[16] The committee report accompanying P.L. 97-72 stated the long-standing position of Congress with regard to health care for Filipino veterans:

> There is little doubt that in 1948 when Congress enacted P.L. 80-865, authorizing a 5-year grant program to provide medical benefits to Filipino veterans with service-connected illnesses, including the authorization for constructing and equipping a hospital in Luzon, it intended that this program be temporary and that the Philippine government would eventually assume responsibility for funding the program and operations of the hospital.... These grants were renewed for an additional 5 years in 1954, but on a decreasing annual scale of payments (P.L. 83-421). The Committee report on this bill stated that progressively reducing these grants over five years was to make clear the intent of Congress that the Philippine government would be expected to gradually assume full responsibility for the hospital.... However, because of the moral obligation of the United States to provide care for Filipino veterans and the concern that the Philippine government would not be able to maintain a high standard of medical care to these veterans if assistance by the United States were withheld, this program was extended in 5-year increments through [FY] 1978. P.L. 89- 612, enacted in September 1966, expanded the program to include medical care for nonservice-connected disabilities if the veteran were unable to defray the expense of medical care and included New Philippine Scouts in the coverage.[17]

Furthermore, P.L. 97-72 gave the VA the authority to contract for the care and treatment of U.S. veterans in the VMMC, and to provide grant authority of $500,000 per year for a period of five years for making grants to the VMMC to assist in the replacement and upgrading of equipment and the rehabilitation of the physical plant and facilities of the center.

The grant program was further authorized by making amendments to the grant amount and the time frame for entering into contracts by the following acts:

- P.L. 100-687, enacted on November 18, 1988;
- Department of Veterans Affairs Health-Care Personnel Act of 1991 (P.L. 102-40), enacted on May 7, 1991;
- Veterans' Benefits Improvement Act of 1991 (P.L. 102-86), enacted on August 14, 1991; and
- Veterans Health Care Act of 1992 (P.L. 102-585), enacted on November 4, 1992.

In 1993, the VA discontinued referrals of U.S. veterans to the VMMC, because the VA determined that the VMMC was not providing a reasonable standard of care. Until this time, the VMMC had been the primary contract hospital for the VA in the Philippines. Because of this change in the referral process, the grant-in-aid funding for the VMMC was last authorized by P.L. 102-585 through September 30, 1994, and the program was allowed to expire. However, Congress continued to appropriate funds for the program through September 30, 1996.[18] During a tour of the VMMC in May 2006, the VA Secretary announced that "the VMMC will receive a grant of $500,000, or approximately 25.5 million pesos, from the U.S. government to help the institution purchase additional equipment and materials for the treatment of Filipino veterans."[19] The VA currently provides grants of equipment under the authority of 38 U.S.C. § 1731.

Non-Health Care Benefits

P.L. 82-21

Enacted on April 25, 1951, P.L. 82-21 authorized funeral and burial benefits, including burial flags, for Commonwealth Army veterans residing in the Philippines (at half the rate of U.S. veterans). These benefits were not extended to New Philippine Scouts.

P.L. 89-613

Enacted on September 30, 1966, P.L. 89-613 extended dependents' and survivors' education assistance to include children of Commonwealth Army veterans and New Philippine Scouts. These benefits were made payable at half the rate of the benefits for children of U.S. veterans.

P.L. 89-641

As a result of a Joint Republic of the Philippines-U.S. Commission study of Philippine veterans' problems, P.L. 89-641, enacted on October 11, 1966 changed how benefits were to be computed by providing for the payment of benefits in pesos based on pesos being equal in value to U.S. 50 cents for each U.S. dollar authorized. In 1978, testifying before the Senate Committee on Appropriations, the General Accounting Office (now the Government Accountability Office) stated that

> [T]he intent of the 1966 law was apparently to restore Philippines beneficiaries to approximately their situation in 1946, taking into account the changes occurring in the economies and living standards in the Philippines and the U.S. since 1946. Since the law was enacted, however, legislative increases and devaluations of the peso have provided Filipino veterans with

undue increases in benefits and has resulted in Filipino veterans achieving much higher levels of benefits than their counterparts in the U.S.[20]

BENEFIT CHANGES SINCE 1998

Foster Care Independence Act of 1999 (P.L. 106-169)

Enacted on December 12, 1999, P.L. 106-169 expanded U.S. income-based benefits to certain World War II veterans, including Filipino veterans, who served in the organized military forces of the Philippines while those forces were in the service of the U.S. Armed Forces. Until the enactment of this act, recipients of Supplemental Security Income (SSI)[21] were generally required to reside in the United States to maintain their eligibility. This law enabled eligible Filipino veterans to return to the Philippines and retain 75% of their SSI benefits.

The Departments of Veterans Affairs and Housing and Urban Development, and Independent Agencies Appropriations Act, 2001 (P.L. 106-377)

Enacted on October 27, 2000, P.L. 106-477 changed the rate of compensation payments to veterans of the Commonwealth Army of the Philippines and veterans of Recognized Guerrilla Forces who lawfully reside in the United States. P.L. 106-377 also authorized the VA to provide hospital care, medical services, and nursing home care to these two veterans groups, similar to care and services available to U.S veterans. In order to receive these benefits, they were required to be legal permanent residents of the United States and be receiving VA disability compensation. P.L. 106-377, also authorized outpatient care at the Manila VA Outpatient Clinic to service-connected U.S. veterans for their nonservice-connected disabilities.[22] Prior to the enactment of P.L. 106-377, the VA was limited to providing outpatient treatment for U.S. veterans in the Philippines only for their service-connected conditions.

The Veterans Benefits and Health Care Improvement Act of 2000 (P.L. 106-419)

Enacted on November 1, 2000, P.L. 106-419 changed the amount of monetary burial benefits that the VA will pay to survivors of veterans of the Philippine Commonwealth Army and Recognized Guerrilla Forces who lawfully reside in the United States at the time of death.

The Veterans Health Care, Capital Asset, and Business Improvement Act of 2003 (P.L. 108-170)

Enacted on December 6, 2003, P.L. 108-170 authorized the VA to provide hospital care, nursing home care, and outpatient medical services to Filipino Commonwealth Army veterans, veterans of Recognized Guerrilla Forces, and New Philippine Scouts. Currently, these groups of veterans are eligible for hospital care, nursing home care, and outpatient medical services within the United States.

The Veterans Benefits Act of 2003 (P.L. 108-183)

Enacted on December 16, 2003, P.L. 108-183 added service in the New Philippine Scouts as qualifying service for payment of disability compensation, dependency, and indemnity compensation (DIC) and monetary burial benefits at the full-dollar rate, and provided for payment of DIC at the full-dollar rate to survivors of veterans of the Philippine Commonwealth Army and Recognized Guerrilla Forces who lawfully reside in the United States.

It should be noted that veterans of the U.S. Armed Forces have the same entitlement to monetary benefits in the Philippines that they would have in the United States, with the exception of home loans and related programs, which are not available in the Philippines.

Table 1 provides a summary of benefits currently available to Filipino veterans and survivors by category of service (Regular Philippine Scouts, Commonwealth Army of the Philippines, Recognized Guerilla Forces, and New Philippine Scouts).

LEGISLATION IN THE 110TH CONGRESS

H.R. 760 and S. 57 would have eliminated the distinction between the Regular or "Old" Philippine Scouts and the other three groups of veterans—Commonwealth Army of the Philippines, Recognized Guerrilla Forces, and New Philippine Scouts—making them all fully eligible for VA benefits similar to those received by U.S. veterans. H.R. 760 was reported out of committee. S. 66 would have required the Secretary of the Army to validate claims by Filipinos that they performed military service in the Philippine Islands during World War II that would qualify them for benefits under U.S. law and issue a certificate of service.

S. 1315, as passed by the Senate, incorporated provisions from S. 57. S. 1315 would have altered current law to deem certain service with Philippine forces during World War II as active service and establish rates for the Improved Pension and the Death Pension for veterans who served with the Philippine forces and their survivors living outside the United States. Under the provisions of S. 1315, single Filipino veterans living outside the United States would receive $3,600 a year, married veterans would receive $4,500 a year, and veterans' survivors would receive $2,400 a year. However, under the bill, veterans living outside the United States who are eligible for, or receiving, the Social Security benefit for World War II veterans living overseas would not be not eligible for the new Improved Pension rates. The bill also would not have applied the current income or net worth limitations for the Improved Pension and the Death Pension for veterans who served with the Philippine forces and their survivors living outside the United States. In addition, the bill would not have required any veteran who served with the Philippine forces or their survivors receiving other federal benefits at the time of enactment to apply for the Improved Pension or the Death Pension if receiving the new benefits would have made them ineligible for their other federal benefits or reduced the amount of their other federal benefits. S. 1315 provided that disability compensation (for service-connected disabilities) would be paid to all recipients at the same rate regardless of residence, while maintaining the general payment rate of 50 cents per dollar for other benefits to Filipino veterans and survivors living outside the United States.[23] On September 22, 2008, the House passed an amended version of S. 1315 that did not contain the Filipino benefit provisions.

Table 1. Filipino Veterans and Survivors, Eligibility for VA Benefits

Veterans' Benefit	Regular, or "Old," Philippine Scouts		Commonwealth Army of the Philippines		Recognized Guerrilla Forces		New Philippine Scouts	
	Living in the U.S[a]	Living Outside the U.S.	Living in the U.S[a]	Living Outside the U.S.	Living in the U.S[a]	Living Outside the U.S.	Living in the U.S[a]	Living Outside the U.S.
Compensation for service-connected disability	Yes	Yes	Yes	Yes[b]	Yes	Yes[b]	Yes	Yes[b]
Dependency and Indemnity Compensation/ DIC (survivors)	Yes	Yes	Yes	Yes[b]	Yes	Yes[b]	Yes	Yes[b]
Medical care	Yes	No[c]	Yes	No	Yes	No	Yes	No
Education benefits[d]	Yes	Yes	No	No	No	No	No	No
Education benefits for children	Yes	Yes	Yes	Yes[b]	Yes	Yes[b]	Yes	Yes[b]
Pension for nonservice-connected disability	Yes	Yes	No	No	No	No	No	No
Death pension (survivors)	Yes	Yes	No	No	No	No	No	No
Burial allowance	Yes	Yes	Yes	Yes[b]	Yes	Yes[b]	Yes	Yes[b]
Burial flag	Yes	Yes	Yes	Yes	Yes	Yes	Yes	Yes
Burial in a national cemetery	Yes	Yes	Yes	No	Yes	No	Yes	No
Clothing allowance	Yes	Yes	Yes	Yes[b]	Yes	Yes[b]	Yes	Yes[b]
Guaranteed housing loans	Yes	No[e]	No	No	No	No	No	No

Table 1. (Continued)

Veterans' Benefit	Regular, or "Old," Philippine Scouts		Commonwealth Army of the Philippines		Recognized Guerrilla Forces		New Philippine Scouts	
	Living in the U.S[a]	Living Outside the U.S.	Living in the U.S[a]	Living Outside the U.S.	Living in the U.S[a]	Living Outside the U.S.	Living in the U.S[a]	Living Outside the U.S.
Small business loans	Yes	No[e]	No	No	No	No	No	No
Veterans Employment Training Service (VETS)[f]	Yes	Yes[g]	No	No	No	No	No	No
Adaptive housing grants	Yes	No[e]	No	No	No	No	No	No
Adaptive vehicle grants	Yes	Yes	No	No	No	No	No	No

Source: Table prepared by the Congressional Research Service (CRS) based on information provided by the Department of Veterans Affairs.

a. Living in the United States as a U.S. citizen or legal resident.

b. Benefit is paid at the rate of 50 cents per $1.

c .Regular or "Old" Philippine Scouts residing in the Philippines are only eligible for hospital care for treatment of service-connected conditions. In addition, they are authorized to receive outpatient care in facilities other than the Manila VA Outpatient Clinic for service-connected conditions only. Finally, if they are service-connected, they are eligible to receive care for service-connected and nonservice-connected conditions at the Manila VA Outpatient Clinic based on resources available at the clinic.

d. The time period for using education benefits has expired.

e. Certain benefits are not available to any U.S. veteran living overseas.

f. This program did not exist in 1946.

g. Must be enrolled in a degree granting college or university.

H.R. 6897, as passed by the House on September 23, 2008, would have provided a one-time payment to Filipino veterans who served in the Commonwealth Army of the Philippines, Recognized Guerrilla Forces, and New Philippine Scouts. The payment would be $15,000 for U.S. citizens and $9,000 for non-U.S citizens. Payments are made from the Filipino Veterans Equity Compensation Fund and are subject to funds being available (appropriated). P.L. 110-329 appropriated $198 million for the Filipino Veterans Equity Compensation Fund.

LEGISLATION IN THE 111TH CONGRESS

The American Recovery and Reinvestment Act of 2009 (ARRA, P.L. 111-5) authorizes a onetime payment from the Filipino Veterans Equity Compensation Fund to Filipino veterans who served in the Commonwealth Army of the Philippines, Recognized Guerrilla Forces, and New Philippine Scouts. The one-time payment is $15,000 for U.S. citizens and $9,000 for non-U.S citizens. Filipino veterans currently receiving benefits will continue to receive those benefits. The one-time payment does not impact eligibility for federally assisted programs. The one-time payment is considered a settlement for all future claims for benefits based on service in the Commonwealth Army of the Philippines, Recognized Guerrilla Forces, and New Philippine Scouts. The exception is that a veteran may receive benefits that the veteran would have been eligible for based on the laws in effect on the day before enactment (September 17, 2009).

End Notes

[1] 38 U.S.C. §101(6).
[2] 38 C.F.R. §3.40(a).
[3] 38 C.F.R. §3.40(d).
[4] 38 C.F.R. §3.40(b).
[5] The term "service-connected" means, with respect to disability, that such disability was incurred or aggravated in the line of duty in the active military, naval, or air service. The VA determines whether veterans have service-connected disabilities, and for those with such disabilities, assigns ratings from 0 to 100% based on the severity of the disability. Percentages are assigned in increments of 10%.
[6] P.L. 79-301; 60 Stat. 14.
[7] Ibid; now codified at 38 U.S.C. §107.

[8] For example, if a veteran who was a member of the U.S. Armed Forces received $50 for a benefit, a veteran who was a member of the Commonwealth Army would receive 50 pesos for the same benefit.

[9] In 1942, the Solicitor of the VA ruled that members of the Commonwealth Army called into the service of the United States by the President's order of July 26, 1941, were eligible for benefits under the Veterans' National Life Insurance Act. In 1945, General Omar Bradley, then Director of the Veterans' Administration, expressed an opinion to the Senate Appropriations Committee that the term "veterans" included these Commonwealth Army veterans. *Filipino American Veterans and Dependents Association v. United States of America*, 391 F. Supp. 1314 (N.D. Cal. 1974).

[10] U.S . Congress, Senate Committee on Appropriations, Subcommittee on Deficiency, Hearings on H.R. 5604, 79th Cong., 2nd sess., March 25, 1946, p. 29.

[11] U.S. Congress, Senate Committee on Appropriations, Subcommittee on Deficiency, Hearings on H.R. 5604, 79th Cong., 2nd sess., March 25, 1946, p. 61.

[12] U.S. Congress, House Committee on Veterans' Affairs, *Medical Care of Veterans,* Committee print, 90th Cong., 1st sess., April 17, 1967. House Committee print no. 4, p. 384.

[13] See http://server.pvao.mil.ph/vmmc.html.

[14] This law defined "Commonwealth Army Veterans" as "persons who served before July 1, 1946, in the organized military forces of the Government of the Philippines, while such forces were in the service of the Armed Forces pursuant to the military order of the President dated July 26, 1941, including among such military forces organized guerrilla forces under commanders appointed, designated, or subsequently recognized by the Commander in Chief, Southwest Pacific Area, or another competent authority in the Army of the United States, and who were discharged or released from such service under conditions other than dishonorable."

[15] This language contained in P.L. 85-461 was restated in P.L. 85-857, which consolidated the laws of the Veterans' Administration.

[16] U.S. Congress, House Committee on Veterans' Affairs, *Veterans' Health Care, Training, and Small Business Loan Act of 1981.* Report to accompany H.R. 3499. 97th Cong., 1st sess., H.Rept. 97-79.

[17] Ibid.

[18] Department of Veterans Affairs and Housing and Urban Development, Independent Agencies Appropriations Act, 1995 (P.L. 103-327).

[19] U.S. Embassy Press Release, "Medical Center to Benefit from 25-Million Peso Grant; Hosts Visiting U.S. Secretary of Veterans Affairs," May 1, 2006.

[20] U.S. Congress, Senate Committee on Appropriations, Veterans Administration Benefits Programs in the Republic of the Philippines, Hearings, 95th Cong., 1st sess., August 31, 1977 (Washington: GPO, 1978).

[21] This program is administered by the Social Security Administration.

[22] 38 U.S.C. Section 1724(e). This clinic refers to the Manila VA Clinic, which is located at 2201 Roxas Boulevard, Pasay City, Metro Manila, and not to the VMMC.

[23] To offset the cost of the expanded pension benefits for Filipino veterans and survivors, S. 1315 would have denied, to veterans over age 65 receiving the Improved Pension benefit, the special monthly pension (for housebound or aid and attendance) unless the veteran also met the disability requirements for the Improved Pension program. This would have overturned a decision of the United States Court of Appeals for Veterans Claims in *Hartness* v. *Nicholson*, 20 VET. App. 216 (2006).

In: Republic of the Philippines and U.S. Relations ISBN: 978-1-61668-951-3
Editor: Margaret R. Voigt

Chapter 3

COUNTRY PROFILE: PHILIPPINES*

Library of Congress - Federal Research Division

COUNTRY

Formal Name: Republic of the Philippines (Republika ng Pilipinas).

Short Form: Philippines (Pilipinas).

Term for Citizen(s): Filipino(s).

Capital: Manila.

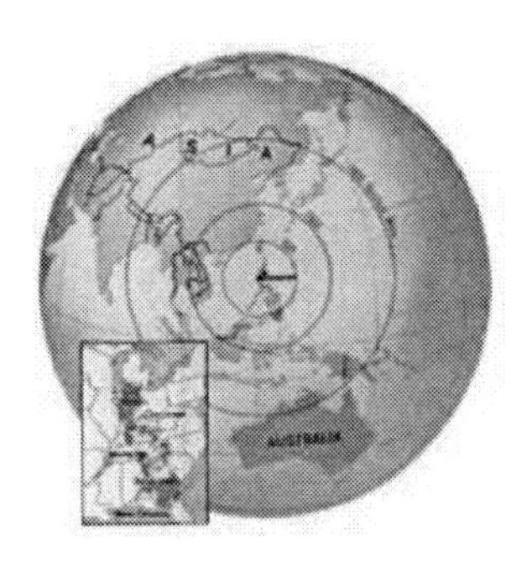

* This is an edited, reformatted and augmented version of a Library of Congress publication dated March 2006.

Major Cities: Located on Luzon Island, Metropolitan Manila, including the adjacent Quezon City and surrounding suburbs, is the largest city in the Philippines, with about 12 million people, or nearly 14 percent of the total population. Other large cities include Cebu City on Cebu Island and Davao City on Mindanao Island.

Independence: The Philippines attained independence from Spain on June 12, 1898, and from the United States on July 4, 1946.

Public Holidays: New Year's Day (January 1), Holy Thursday (also called Maundy Thursday, movable date in March or April), Good Friday (movable date in March or April), Araw ng Kagitingan (Day of Valor, commonly called Bataan Day outside of the Philippines, April 9), Labor Day (May 1), Independence Day (June 12), National Heroes Day (last Sunday of August), Bonifacio Day (celebration of the birthday of Andres Bonifacio, November 30), Eid al Fitr (the last day of Ramadan, movable date), Christmas Day (December 25), Rizal Day (the date of the execution by the Spanish of José Rizal in 1896, December 30).

Flag: The flag of the Philippines has two equal horizontal bands of blue (top) and red with a white equilateral triangle based on the hoist side; in the center of the triangle is a yellow sun with eight primary rays (each containing three individual rays), and in each corner of the triangle is a small yellow five-pointed star.

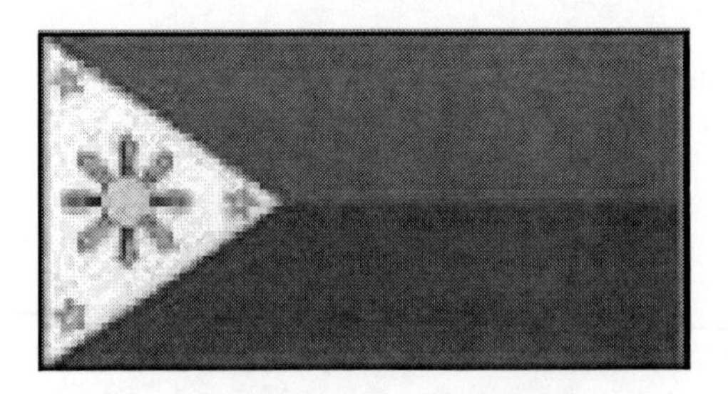

HISTORICAL BACKGROUND

Early History: The Philippine archipelago was settled at least 30,000 years ago, when migrations from the Indonesian archipelago and elsewhere are believed to have occurred. Additional migrations took place over the next millennia. Over time, social and political organization developed and evolved in the widely scattered islands. The basic unit of settlement was the *barangay* (a Malay word for boat that came to be used to denote a communal settlement). Kinship groups were led by a *datu* (chief), and within the *barangay* there were broad social divisions consisting of nobles, freemen, and dependent and landless agricultural workers and slaves. Over the centuries, Indo-Malay migrants were joined by Chinese traders. A major development in the early period was the introduction of Islam to the Philippines by traders and proselytizers from the Indonesian islands. By A.D. 1500, Islam had been established in the Sulu Archipelago and spread from there to Mindanao; it reached the Manila area by 1565. In the midst of the introduction of Islam came the introduction of Christianity, with the arrival of the Spanish.

Spanish Control: Ferdinand Magellan was the first European recorded to have landed in the Philippines. He arrived in March 1521 during his circumnavigation of the globe. He claimed land for the king of Spain but was killed by a local chief. Following several more Spanish expeditions, the first permanent settlement was established in Cebu in 1565. After defeating a local Muslim ruler, the Spanish set up their capital at Manila in 1571, and they named their new colony after King Philip II of Spain. In doing so, the Spanish sought to acquire a share in the lucrative spice trade, develop better contacts with China and Japan, and gain converts to Christianity. Only the third objective was eventually realized. As with other Spanish colonies, church and state became inseparably linked in carrying out Spanish objectives. Several Roman Catholic religious orders were assigned the responsibility of Christianizing the local population. The civil administration built upon the traditional village organization and used traditional local leaders to rule indirectly for Spain. Through these efforts, a new cultural community was developed, but Muslims (known as Moros by the Spanish) and upland tribal peoples remained detached and alienated.

Trade in the Philippines centered around the "Manila galleons," which sailed from Acapulco on the west coast of Mexico (New Spain) with shipments of silver bullion and minted coin that were exchanged for return cargoes of Chinese goods, mainly silk textiles and porcelain. There was no direct trade with Spain and little exploitation of indigenous natural resources. Most investment was in the galleon trade. But, as this trade thrived, another unwelcome element was introduced— sojourning Chinese entrepreneurs and service providers.

During the Seven Years' War (1756–63), British East India Company forces captured Manila. Although the Philippines was returned to Spain at the end of the war, the British occupation marked the beginning of the end of the old order. Rebellions broke out in the north, and while the Spanish were busy fighting the British, Moros raided from the south. The Chinese community, resentful of Spanish discrimination, supported the British with laborers and armed men. The restoration of Spanish rule brought reforms aimed at promoting the economic development of the islands and making them independent of subsidies from New Spain. The galleon trade ceased in 1815, and from that date onward the Royal Company of the Philippines, which had been chartered in 1785, promoted direct and tariff-free trade between the islands and Spain. Cash crops were cultivated for trade with Europe and Latin America, but profits diminished after Spain's Latin American colonies became independent in the 1810s and 1820s. In 1834 the Royal Company of the Philippines was abolished, and free trade was formally recognized. With its excellent harbor, Manila became an open port for Asian, European, and North American traders. In 1873 additional ports were opened to foreign commerce, and by the late nineteenth century three crops—tobacco, abaca, and sugar—dominated Philippine exports.

Rise of Nationalism: Also in the late nineteenth century, Chinese immigration, now with official approval, increased, and Chinese mestizos became a feature in Filipino social and economic life. So, too, did the growing Filipino native elite class of *ilustrados* (literally, enlightened ones), who became increasingly receptive to liberal and democratic ideas. Conservative Catholic friars continued to dominate the Spanish establishment, however. They resisted the inclusion of native clergy and were economically secure, with their large land holdings and control of churches, schools, and other establishments. Despite the bias against native priests, brothers, and nuns, some members of Filipino religious orders became prominent to the point of leading local religious movements and even insurrections against the establishment. Additionally, *ilustrados* returning from education and exile abroad brought new ideas that merged with folk religion to spur a national resistance.

One of the early nationalist leaders was José Rizal, a physician, scientist, scholar, and writer. His writings as a member of the Propaganda Movement (intellectually active, upper-class Filipino reformers) had a considerable impact on the awakening of the Filipino national consciousness. His books were banned, and he lived in self-imposed exile. Rizal returned from overseas in 1892 to found the Liga Filipina (Philippine League), a national, nonviolent political organization, but he was arrested and exiled and the league dissolved. One result was the split of the nationalist movement between the reform-minded *ilustrados* and a more revolutionary and independence- minded plebeian constituency. Many of the latter joined the Katipunan, a secret society founded by Andres Bonifacio in 1892 and committed to winning national independence. By 1896, the year the Katipunan rose in revolt against Spain, it had 30,000 members. Although Rizal, who had again returned to the Philippines, was not a member of the Katipunan, he was arrested and executed on December 30, 1896, for his alleged role in the rebellion. With Rizal's martyrdom, the rebels, led by Emilio Aguinaldo as president, were filled with new determination. Spanish troops defeated the insurgents, however, and Aguinaldo and his government went into exile in Hong Kong in December 1897.

When the Spanish-American War broke out in April 1898, Spain's fleet was easily defeated at Manila. Aguinaldo returned, and his 12,000 troops kept the Spanish forces bottled up in Manila until U.S. troops landed. The Spanish cause was doomed, but the Americans did nothing to accommodate the inclusion of Aguinaldo in the succession. Fighting between American and Filipino troops broke out almost as soon as the Spanish had been defeated. Aguinaldo issued a declaration of independence on June 12, 1898. However, the Treaty of Paris, signed on December 10, 1898, by the United States and Spain, ceded the Philippines, Guam, and Puerto Rico to the United States, recognized Cuban independence, and gave US$20 million to Spain. A revolutionary congress convened at Malolos, north of Manila, promulgated a constitution on January 21, 1899, and inaugurated Aguinaldo as president of the new republic two days later. Hostilities broke out in February 1899, and by March 1901 Aguinaldo had been captured and his forces defeated. Despite Aguinaldo's call to his compatriots to lay down their arms, insurgent resistance continued until 1903. The Moros, suspicious of both the Christian Filipino insurgents and the Americans, remained largely neutral, but eventually their own armed resistance had to be subjugated, and Moro territory was placed under U.S. military rule until 1914.

United States Rule: U.S. rule over the Philippines had two phases. The first phase was from 1898 to 1935, during which time Washington defined its colonial mission as one of tutelage and preparing the Philippines for eventual independence. Political organizations developed quickly, and the popularly elected Philippine Assembly (lower house) and the U.S.-appointed Philippine

Commission (upper house) served as a bicameral legislature. The *ilustrados* formed the Federalista Party, but their statehood platform had limited appeal. In 1905 the party was renamed the National Progressive Party and took up a platform of independence. The Nacionalista Party was formed in 1907 and dominated Filipino politics until after World War II. Its leaders were not ilustrados. Despite their "immediate independence" platform, the party leaders participated in a collaborative leadership with the United States. A major development emerging in the post- World War I period was resistance to elite control of the land by tenant farmers, who were supported by the Socialist Party and the Communist Party of the Philippines. Tenant strikes and occasional violence occurred as the Great Depression wore on and cash-crop prices collapsed.

The second period of United States rule—from 1936 to 1946—was characterized by the establishment of the Commonwealth of the Philippines and occupation by Japan during World War II. Legislation passed by the U.S. Congress in 1934 provided for a 10-year period of transition to independence. The country's first constitution was framed in 1934 and overwhelmingly approved by plebiscite in 1935, and Manuel Quezon was elected president of the commonwealth. Quezon later died in exile in 1944 and was succeeded by Vice President Sergio Osme a. Japan attacked the Philippines on December 8, 1941, and occupied Manila on January 2, 1942. Tokyo set up an ostensibly independent republic, which was opposed by underground and guerrilla activity that eventually reached large-scale proportions. A major element of the resistance in the Central Luzon area was furnished by the Huks (short for Hukbalahap, or People's Anti-Japanese Army). Allied forces invaded the Philippines in October 1944, and the Japanese surrendered on September 2, 1945.

Early Independence Period: World War II had been demoralizing for the Philippines, and the islands suffered from rampant inflation and shortages of food and other goods. Various trade and security issues with the United States also remained to be settled before Independence Day. The Allied leaders wanted to purge officials who collaborated with the Japanese during the war and to deny them the right to vote in the first postwar elections. Commonwealth President Osme a, however, countered that each case should be tried on its own merits. The successful Liberal Party presidential candidate, Manual Roxas, was among those collaborationists. Independence from the United States came on July 4, 1946, and Roxas was sworn in as the first president. The economy remained highly dependent on U.S. markets, and the

United States also continued to maintain control of 23 military installations. A bilateral treaty was signed in March 1947 by which the United States continued to provide military aid, training, and matériel. Such aid was timely, as the Huk guerrillas rose again, this time against the new government. They changed their name to the People's Liberation Army (Hukbong Mapagpalaya ng Bayan) and demanded political participation, disbandment of the military police, and a general amnesty. Negotiations failed, and a rebellion began in 1950 with communist support. The aim was to overthrow the government. The Huk movement dissipated into criminal activities by 1951, as the better-trained and -equipped Philippine armed forces and conciliatory government moves toward the peasants offset the effectiveness of the Huks.

Populist Ramón Magsaysay of the Nacionalista Party was elected president in 1953 and embarked on widespread reforms that benefited tenant farmers in the Christian north while exacerbating hostilities with the Muslim south. The remaining Huk leaders were captured or killed, and by 1954 the movement had waned. After Magsaysay's death in an airplane crash in 1957, he was succeeded by Vice President Carlos P. Garcia. Garcia was elected in his own right the same year, and he advanced the nationalist theme of "Filipinos First," reaching agreement with the United States to relinquish large areas of land no longer needed for military operations. In 1961 the Liberal Party candidate, Diosdado Macapagal, was elected president. Subsequent negotiations with the United States over base rights led to considerable anti-American feelings and demonstrations. Macapagal sought closer relations with his Southeast Asian neighbors and convened a summit with the leaders of Indonesia and Malaysia in the hope of developing a spirit of consensus, which did not emerge.

The Marcos Era: Nacionalista Party leader Ferdinand Marcos came to dominate the political scene for the next two decades, beginning with his election to the presidency in 1965. During his first term, Marcos initiated ambitious public works projects that improved the general quality of life while providing generous pork-barrel benefits for his friends. Marcos perceived that his promised land reform program would alienate the politically all-powerful landowner elite, and thus it was never forcefully implemented. He lobbied strenuously for economic and military aid from the United States while resisting significant involvement in the Second Indochina War (1954–75). In 1967 the Philippines became a founding member of the Association of Southeast Asian Nations (ASEAN). Marcos became the first president to be reelected (in 1969), but early in his second term economic growth slowed, optimism faded, and the crime rate increased. In addition, a new communist insurgency, this time—starting in 1 968—led by the new Communist Party of the Philippines-Marxist-Leninist and its military arm, the New People's Army, was on the rise. In 1969 the Moro National Liberation Front was founded and conducted an insurgency in Muslim areas. Political violence blamed on leftists, but probably initiated by government agents provocateurs, led Marcos to suspend habeas corpus as a prelude to martial law.

Marcos declared martial law on September 21, 1972, and did not lift it until January 17, 1981. During this time, he called for self-sacrifice and an end to the old society. However, in the "New Society" Marcos's cronies and his wife, former movie actress Imelda Romualdez-Marcos, wilfully engaged in rampant corruption. With her husband's support, Imelda Marcos built her own power base. She became governor of Metropolitan Manila and minister of human settlements. The previously nonpolitical armed forces became highly politicized, with high- ranking positions being given to Marcos loyalists. In 1979 the United States reaffirmed Philippine sovereignty over U.S. military bases and continued to provide military and economic aid to the Marcos regime. When martial law was lifted in 1981 and a "New Republic" proclaimed, little had actually changed, and Marcos easily won reelection.

The beginning of the end of the Marcos era occurred when his chief political rival, Liberal Party leader Benigno "Ninoy" Aquino, who had been jailed by Marcos for eight years, was assassinated as he disembarked from an airplane at the Manila International Airport on August 21, 1983, following medical treatment in the United States. Marcos cronies were charged with this crime but were acquitted. Aquino, however, became a martyr and his murder the focus of popular indignation against a corrupt regime. The Catholic Church, a coalition of old political opposition groups, the business elite, the left wing, and even factions of the armed forces all began to exert pressure on the regime. There also was foreign pressure and, feeling confident with the support given by the Reagan White House, Marcos called a "snap" presidential election for February 7, 1986. When the Marcos-dominated National Assembly proclaimed Marcos the winner, Cardinal Jaime Sin and key military leaders (including Minister of Defense Juan Ponce Enrile and acting Chief of Staff of the Armed Forces Lieutenant General Fidel V. Ramos) rallied around the apparent majority vote winner, Aquino's widow, Corazon Cojuango Aquino. The People Power Movement—a popular uprising of priests, nuns, ordinary citizens, and children, supported by defecting military units—ousted Marcos on the day of his inauguration (February 25, 1986) and brought Aquino to power in an almost bloodless revolution.

The Aquino Years and Beyond: Corazon Aquino had wide popular support but no political organization. Her vice president, Salvador H. "Doy" Laurel, had an organization but little popular support. Enrile and Ramos also had large stakes in what they saw as a coalition government. The coalition unraveled quickly, and there were several attempts, including unsuccessful military coups, to oust Aquino. She survived her fractious term, however, and was succeeded in the 1992 election by Ramos, who had served loyally as chief of staff of the armed forces and secretary of national defense under Aquino.

President Ramos worked at coalition building and overcoming the divisiveness of the Aquino years. Mutinous right-wing soldiers, communist insurgents, and Muslim separatists were convinced to cease their armed activities against the government and were granted amnesty. In an act of reconciliation, Ramos allowed the remains of Ferdinand Marcos—he had died in exile in the United States in 1989—to be returned to the Philippines for burial in 1993. Efforts by supporters of Ramos to gain passage of an amendment that would allow him to run for a second term were met with large-scale protests supported by Cardinal Sin and Corazon Aquino, leading Ramos to declare he would not run again.

Joseph Estrada, who had served as Ramos's vice president and enjoyed widespread popularity, was elected president in 1998. Within a year, however, Estrada's popularity declined sharply amid allegations of cronyism and corruption and failure to remedy the problems of poverty. Once again, street rallies supported by Cardinal Sin and Corazon Aquino took place. Then, in 2000 Senate investigators accused Estrada of having accepted bribes from illegal gambling businesses. Following an abortive Senate impeachment trial, growing street protests, and the withdrawal of support by the armed forces, Estrada was forced out of office on January 20, 2001.

Vice President Gloria Macapagal-Arroyo (the daughter of the late President Diosdado Macapagal) was sworn in as Estrada's successor on the day of his departure. Her accession to power was further legitimated by the mid-term congressional and local elections, when her coalition later won an overwhelming victory, but the elections were fraught with allegations of coercion, fraud, and vote buying. Macapagal-Arroyo's initial term in office was marked by fractious coalition politics as well as a military mutiny in Manila in July 2003 that led her to declare a month-long nationwide state of rebellion, as a result of which charges were filed against more than 1,000 individuals. Macapagal-Arroyo had declared in December 2002 that she would not contest the May 2004 presidential election, but she reversed herself in October 2003 and decided to run. She was reelected and sworn in for her own six-year term as president on June 30, 2004. With this new mandate, she was able to move with greater assurance on the political and economic reform agenda that had stalled during her first term in office.

GEOGRAPHY

Location: The Philippines comprises an archipelago of some 7,107 islands located off Southeast Asia, between the South China Sea on the west and the Philippine Sea on the east. The major islands are Luzon in the north, the Visayan Islands in the middle, and Mindanao in the south.

Size: The total area is about 300,000 square kilometers, including about 298,000 square kilometers of land and about 2,000 square kilometers of water. The Philippines stretches about 1,850 kilometers from Y'Ami Island in the north to Sibutu Island in the south and is about 1,000 kilometers at its widest point east to west. The bulk of the population lives on 11 of the 7,107 islands.

Land Boundaries: The Philippines has no land boundaries. Nearby neighbors are Taiwan to the north, Malaysia and Indonesia to the south, Vietnam to the west, and China to the northwest.

Disputed Territory: The Philippines, China, Taiwan, Malaysia, and Vietnam hold conflicting claims to portions of the South China Sea and the Spratly Islands, which are called the Kalayaan (Freedom) Islands in the

Philippines. The Philippines also disputes Malaysia's claim to the state of Sabah.

Length of Coastline: Estimates of the total length of the coastline range from 17,500 kilometers (official Philippine figure) to 36,289 kilometers (U.S. figure).

Maritime Claims: The Philippines claims a territorial sea of up to 100 nautical miles from the nearest coastline, an area that includes the entire Sulu Sea and the northern part of the Celebes Sea. A presidential decree in 1978 announced additional baselines, which in effect extended the territorial sea to claim an area up to 285 nautical miles in breadth in the South China Sea west of Palawan Island. This area encompasses the Spratly Islands. The Philippines also claims its continental shelf to the depth of exploitation and an exclusive economic zone of 200 nautical miles from its baselines.

Topography: The Philippines consists of volcanic islands, including active volcanoes, with mostly mountainous interiors surrounded by flat lowlands and alluvial plains of varying widths along the coasts. The elevation ranges from sea level to the highest point of Mount Apo on Mindanao Island, at 2,954 meters above sea level.

Principal Rivers: The longest river is the Cagayan (Río Grande de Cagayan) on Luzon, about 350 kilometers in length. Other principal rivers on Luzon include the Abra, Bicol, Chico, and Pampanga. The Pasig River is only about 25 kilometers in length but serves as the main waterway, flowing between Laguna de Bay, the largest freshwater lake in the Philippines, through metropolitan Manila to Manila Bay. Principal rivers on Mindanao include the Mindanao River (known as the Pulangi River in its upper reaches), and the Agusan. The St. Paul River on Palawan is an eight-kilometer-long underground river.

Climate: The Philippines has a tropical marine climate, with the northeast monsoon, which produces a cool, dry season from December to February, and the southwest monsoon, which brings rain and high temperatures from May to October. Between March and May, hot, dry weather prevails. Temperatures in Manila range from 21°C to 32°C, with an average annual temperature of 27°C. Temperatures elsewhere in the Philippines have been recorded at more than 37°C. The average monthly humidity ranges from 71 percent in March to 85 percent in September. Annual rainfall is heavy but varies widely throughout the Philippines, ranging from 965 millimeters in some sheltered valleys and the southern tip of the island of Mindanao to 5,000 millimeters along the mountainous east coasts of the islands of Luzon, Samar, and the northern tip of Mindanao. The Philippines lies astride the typhoon belt and experiences 15 to 20 typhoons a year from July through October, of which five or six may cause serious destruction and death.

Natural Resources: The major natural mineral resources include coal, cobalt, copper, chromite, gold, gypsum, iron, natural gas, nickel, petroleum, salt, silver, and sulfur. There are lesser deposits of bauxite, lead, mercury, molybdenum, and zinc. Other important resources are geothermal and hydroelectric power, fish, and timber.

Land Use: Out of a total land area of about 300,000 square kilometers, about 92,000 square kilometers are farmland, and about 72,000 square kilometers are forest land, including 65,000 square kilometers of public land and 7,000 square kilometers of privately owned land. Forest area fell steadily from 270,000 square kilometers in 1900 to 80,000 square kilometers in 1970 and to 54,000 square kilometers in 1985. Although forest area subsequently grew from its low in 1985 to its current level in 2004, deforestation is still a major problem. According to the agricultural census of 2002, the number of farms decreased from 4.6 million in 1991 to 4.5 million in 2002, and farm area declined during the same period, from about 100,000 square kilometers in 1991 to its current level.

Environmental Factors: The Philippines is prone to natural disasters, particularly typhoons, floods, landslides, volcanic eruptions, earthquakes, and tsunamis, lying as it does astride the typhoon belt, in the active volcanic region known as the "Pacific Ring of Fire," and in the geologically unstable region between the Pacific and Eurasian tectonic plates. The Philippines also suffers major human-caused environmental degradation aggravated by a high annual population growth rate, including loss of agricultural lands, deforestation, soil erosion, air and water pollution, improper disposal of solid and toxic wastes, loss of coral reefs, mismanagement and abuse of coastal resources, and overfishing.

Time Zone: The Philippines is in one time zone (Asia/Manila), 8 hours ahead of Greenwich Mean Time.

SOCIETY

Population: The total population of the Philippines was 76.5 million, evenly divided between males and females, at the last census in May 2000. The Philippine National Statistics Office estimated that the total population reached 85.2 million in 2005. The average annual population growth rate from 1998 to 2004 was 2.1 percent. There has been a continuing trend of internal migration from rural to urban areas since at least 1991. According to the 2000 census, 52 percent of the population lived in rural areas and 48 percent in urban areas, including about 12 percent who lived in the National Capital Region, or Metropolitan Manila. The Philippines has a negligible loss of population as a result of emigration, which was estimated at –1.5 migrants per 1,000 population in 2004.

Demography: As of 2005, 35 percent of the population was 0–14 years of age; 61 percent, 15– 64; and 4 percent, 65 and older. According to 2004 data, the gender ratio for the rising generation was 104 males for every 100 females. The birthrate was 25.8 births per 1,000 population. The death rate was 5.5 deaths per 1,000 population. Infant mortality was 24.2 deaths per 1,000 live births. Life expectancy at birth was 66.7 years for males, 72.6 years for females, and 69.6 years overall. The fertility rate was 3.2 children born per woman.

Ethnic Groups: Christian Malays constitute 91.5 percent of the total population, Muslim Malays 4 percent, Chinese 1.5 percent, and others 3 percent.

Languages: The Philippines has two official languages, Filipino (or Pilipino) and English. Filipino has eight major dialects, in order of use: Tagalog, Cebuano, Ilocano, Hiligaynon or Ilonggo, Bicol, Waray, Pampango, and Pangasinense. Filipino, based on Tagalog, is related to Malay and Indonesian and is part of the Malayo-Polynesian subgroup of the Austronesian language family. Filipino is the common language used between speakers of different native languages, which are closely related but not mutually intelligible. English is used in government and as the medium of instruction in higher education.

Religion: About 83 percent of the population is Roman Catholic; 9 percent Protestant, including Presbyterian, Methodist, Philippine Independent

Church, and Philippine Church of Christ; 5 percent Muslim; and 3 percent Buddhist and other. The constitution guarantees freedom of religion and separation of church and state. But Christianity predominates, and Muslims historically have been marginalized.

Education and Literacy: Six years of primary education are free and compulsory; the four-year secondary education program is free but not compulsory. According to the Department of Education, for the school year 2002–3 a total of 12.9 million students were enrolled in elementary education (about 97 percent of the school-age population), including 12 million in public schools run by local government and 910,000 in private schools. A total of 6 million students were enrolled in secondary education (about 66 percent of the school-age population), including about 4.8 million in public schools and 1.2 million in private schools. In addition, about 2.4 million students were enrolled in higher education. At the end of 2005, the simple literacy rate was estimated at 93.4 percent, while the functional literacy rate was 84.1 percent.

Health: In 2000 the Philippines had about 95,000 physicians, or about 1 per 800 people. In 2001 there were about 1,700 hospitals, of which about 40 percent were government run and 60 percent private, with a total of about 85,000 beds, or about one bed per 900 people. The leading causes of morbidity as of 2002 were diarrhea, bronchitis, pneumonia, influenza, hypertension, tuberculosis, heart disease, malaria, chicken pox, and measles. Cardiovascular diseases account for more than 25 percent of all deaths. According to official estimates, 1,965 cases of human immunodeficiency virus (HIV) were reported in 2003, of which 636 had developed acquired immune deficiency syndrome (AIDS). Other estimates state that there may have been as many as 9,400 people living with HIV/AIDS in 2001.

Expenditures on health in 2002 totaled about US$2.2 billion, or about 2.9 percent of gross domestic product (GDP). Government expenditures on health accounted for only about 15 percent of total health expenditures, 30 percent of per capita health expenditures, and about 0.9 percent of all government spending. Per capita health expenditures in 2002 totaled US$28, of which government spending accounted for US$8. Both total and per capita expenditures on health have continued to decline since at least 1990, leading to a decrease in the share of GDP attributable to health expenditures. The main cause of this decline has been the high population growth rate. The government share of total spending on health also has declined steadily, and with more people, there has been less to spend per person from both the government and private sectors.

Welfare: The Philippines' social security system was established in 1957 and is compulsory for all employees, public and private. Retirement is compulsory at age 65 but optional at 60. An employees' compensation program, added in 1975, pays double compensation for work-related death, injury, or illness to employees who are not self-employed. The Philippine Health Insurance Corporation was established in 1995 to administer the National Health Insurance Program, with the stated goal of providing universal coverage. Annual premiums are about US$22. Retirees who have reached the age of 65, or who are older than 60 but not yet 65 and have already paid 120 monthly premiums, pay nothing. Depending on their level of income, heads of poorer households may pay the annual premium and have it include three other family members, as well as themselves. Indigents may have their entire premiums paid in part by the national government and in part by their local government. Benefits do not necessarily cover the full costs of medical expenses, and many poor people still cannot afford to pay the difference.

Economy

Overview: The economy of the Philippines is an anomaly in the Asia-Pacific region in that it has lagged behind other economies, such as those of Singapore, South Korea, and Taiwan. From a position as one of the wealthiest countries in Asia after World War II, the Philippines is now one of the poorest. Since the 1970s, which were a relatively prosperous decade, the Philippines has failed to achieve a sustained period of rapid economic growth and has suffered from recurring economic crises. This persistent underperformance has occurred in spite of the Philippines' rich natural and human resources.

The reasons are rooted partly in history, partly in policy. As a legacy of the U.S. colonial period, oligopolies have dominated the economy, particularly in agriculture, where farmland continues to be concentrated in large estates. In the post-World War II period, the Philippines pursued a strategy of import substitution industrialization, whereby domestic goods are substituted for imports. This strategy required protectionist measures, which led to inefficiencies and the misallocation of resources. Although some trade protectionist measures were relaxed in the early twenty-first century, the

Supreme Court continues to support restrictions on foreign ownership of land and other assets in effect since the constitution of 1935. These restrictions, plus widespread graft and corruption, have suppressed inbound foreign direct investment. A historically low rate of taxation—only about 15 percent of gross domestic product (GDP), partly as a result of widespread tax evasion—has led to underinvestment in infrastructure and uneven economic development.

The National Capital Region around Manila, which produces about 36 percent of GDP with only 12 percent of the population, is much more prosperous than rural areas, where much of the population depends on subsistence living. The traditional lack of job opportunities has led many Filipinos to seek employment outside the country, notably in the Persian Gulf states. Remittances to family members back home—equivalent to 10 percent of GDP—have partially offset a relatively low national rate of savings of about 15 to 18 percent, about average for the Organization for Economic Cooperation and Development, but below average for the region. Current account and budget deficits exacerbate the impact of the low savings rate on growth.

Although trade barriers were scaled back, industrial cartels split up, and limited reform measures taken in the late twentieth century, political instability, continuing high levels of corruption, and resistance to reforms by entrenched interests have prevented the Philippines from pursuing a consistent and effective economic course. The industrial sector continues to decline relative to services, an economic bright spot in which the Philippines apparently enjoys a comparative advantage, although some argue that services represent an employer of last resort. In 2005 the services sector accounted for about 53.5 percent of GDP; industry, 31.7 percent; and agriculture, forestry, and fishing, 14.8 percent.

Poverty is a serious problem in the Philippines. In 2003 per capita gross national income was US$1,080, below the US$1,390 average for lower-middle-income countries. Reflecting regional disparities, in 2003 about 11 percent of Filipinos lived on less than US$1 per day and 40 percent on less than US$2 per day, according to the World Bank. The overall poverty rate declined from 33 percent (25.4 million people) in 2000 to 30.4 percent (23.5 million people) in 2003. Poverty is more concentrated in rural than in urban areas.

Gross Domestic Product (GDP): In 2004 the gross domestic product (GDP) was US$84.6 billion, or US$1,150 on a per capita basis. According to purchasing power parity (PPP), however, GDP in 2005 was estimated to be US$451.3 billion, or US$5,100 per capita. In 2004 the Philippines achieved real economic growth of 6 percent, up from 4.5 percent in 2003. However, with the population expanding by more than 2 percent annually—one of the highest rates in Asia—the actual improvement in living standards is modest.

Government Budget: The budget has shown a deficit every year since 1998, but trends in the early twenty-first century are encouraging. In 2004 the deficit was US$3.4 billion, or about 3.9 percent of gross domestic product (GDP), conforming to the government's increasingly stringent targets for the second consecutive year. During 2005, the government expected to begin to close the revenue gap by introducing an expanded value-added tax. However, the tax's introduction was delayed pending resolution of a dispute over its constitutionality, which came on October 18 in a ruling by the Supreme Court. Historically, the persistent budget deficit, the result of overspending and poor collection by the Bureau of Internal Revenue, has placed restraints on economic growth.

Inflation: In 2005 consumer price inflation was 7.6 percent, up from 5.5 percent in 2004 and 3.0 percent in 2003. The rise in inflation reflected the combined impact of a depreciating peso, rising petroleum prices, and tariffs on electric power to offset losses at the state-owned power utility. The introduction of an expanded value-added tax is expected to provide an additional spur to inflation in 2006. Still, inflation remains well below the peak levels approaching 12 percent registered during the Asian financial crisis of 1997–98.

Agriculture, Forestry, and Fishing: The agricultural sector in the Philippines is known for low productivity, as it employs about 36 percent of the labor force but accounts for only 14.8 percent of gross domestic product (GDP). From 1991 to 2002, both the total number of farms and the total area of farmland decreased, respectively, from 4.6 million to 4.5 million farms and from 9.9 million hectares to 9.2 million hectares of farmland. The average size of each farm decreased from 2.2 hectares to 2.0 hectares.

In the first three quarters of 2005, crops accounted for 46.4 percent of the value of all agricultural production, livestock and poultry for 28.8 percent, and fishing for 24.9 percent. Overall agricultural production rose 1.7 percent over the same period in 2004. In order of value, major agricultural products were rice, poultry, livestock, corn, bananas, and coconuts. The national diet consists mainly of rice, fish, and vegetables, with occasional chicken and pork.

Forestry accounts for less than 1 percent of the total labor force and a minuscule share of all agricultural production, but at 72,000 square kilometers, it accounts for about 45 percent of all agricultural lands and about 25 percent of the total national land area. Once a major industry and the leading earner of foreign exchange in the 1 960s, forestry has declined sharply in importance as a result of rapid deforestation. From a position as the world's leading exporter of tropical hardwoods in the 1970s, the Philippines became a net importer of forest products by the 1990s. In 1990 the Department of Environment and Natural Resources announced a 25-year plan for the sustainable development of the nation's forests. The Congress of the Philippines is considering a nationwide ban on logging; such bans already have been introduced in several provinces.

Fishing consists of municipal fishing, which uses no boats at all, rafts, or boats less than three tons; commercial fishing, which uses boats of three tons or more; and aquaculture farms. In 2004 municipal fishing accounted for about 34 percent of the value of all fishing production, 31 percent of the volume, and 85 percent of the fishing labor force. Commercial fishing accounted for 36 percent of the value, 32 percent of the volume, but only 1 percent of the fishing labor force. Aquaculture accounted for 30 percent of the value, 37 percent of the volume, and 14 percent of the fishing labor force.

Mining and Minerals: The Philippines has substantial copper, chromite, and gold deposits, and the country also is rich in many other minerals, including coal, cobalt, gypsum, iron, nickel, silver, and sulfur. There are also lesser deposits, not currently being mined, of bauxite, lead, mercury, molybdenum, and zinc. The latest exploration by the Minerals and Geosciences Bureau in 1996 estimated that the Philippines had 7.1 billion tons of metallic mineral reserves and 51 billion tons of nonmetallic mineral reserves. Of the metallic reserves, copper accounted for 4.8 billion tons, and gold accounted for 110,000 tons. Of the nonmetallic mineral reserves, limestone accounted for 29 billion tons and marble for 8.5 billion tons. The U.S. Department of State estimates that the Philippines possesses untapped mineral wealth of US$840 billion.

One of the world's top producers of chromite, copper, gold, and nickel in the 1970s and 1980s, the Philippines failed to rank in the top 10 worldwide for the production of any of these minerals or precious metals in 2002. With the closing of several major mines, mining has declined as a share of the gross domestic product (GDP) from a high of 30 percent in the industry's heyday to 1 percent in 2003. Aging infrastructure, high production costs, low commodity prices, and environmental concerns contributed to the decline. In 2003 mining employed only 4 percent of the labor force and claimed a negligible part, about 9,000 hectares, of the total land area.

However, the fortunes of the mining industry may be looking up. In 2003 President Gloria Macapagal-Arroyo announced that the government was shifting its policy from "tolerance to promotion of mining." Consistent with the president's policy, in December 2004 the Supreme Court issued a decision upholding the constitutionality of the 1995 Mining Act, which permits foreign companies to obtain mining and energy service contracts with the Philippine government. Following this decision, the local subsidiary of an Australian mining company announced a gold and copper mining service contract. The government hopes that additional foreign investment in the mining industry will be forthcoming.

Industry and Manufacturing: The production of consumer goods dominates the manufacturing sector. The leading industries are processed foods, followed by electrical machinery (mainly semiconductors), petroleum products, coal, chemical products, and garments. Industry accounted for about 32 percent and the manufacturing subsector for 23–24 percent of gross domestic product (GDP) in 2005. The number of persons employed in manufacturing and construction was about 16 percent of the total labor force in 2004.

Energy: In 2004 the Philippines derived 42 percent of its energy from oil; 30 percent from biomass, solar, and wind; 12 percent from coal; 7 percent from geothermal; 5 percent from hydropower; and 4 percent from natural gas. The Energy Development Plan for 2005–14 calls for the country to work toward energy independence by boosting domestic production of oil, gas, and coal and doubling the use of renewable sources of energy.

The Philippines has 152 million barrels of oil reserves and 3.7 trillion cubic feet of natural gas reserves. In 2004 the Philippines produced 25,000 barrels of oil per day, but domestic consumption was about 338,000 barrels per day, which meant that the Philippines was dependent on imports for about 92.5 percent of its needs. Consumption of oil has remained relatively stable so far this decade as the Philippines has met growing energy demand with electricity generated from natural gas produced by the Malampaya field in the South China Sea beginning in 2001. The Malampaya field, which has about 2.6 trillion cubic feet of natural gas reserves, produces about 25,000 barrels per day of natural gas. A deep-water pipeline carries natural gas to an onshore power station. Eventually, three such stations will have a combined capacity of 2,700 megawatts. In 2003 the Philippines consumed 9.6 million short tons of coal, of which 7.4 million tons (77 percent) were imported. The Philippines is the second largest producer of geothermal power in the world after the United States, and geothermal power accounts for about 50 percent of domestic power generation, followed by hydropower, which accounts for about 33 percent. The development of hydropower through the construction of large dams, however, has been controversial. Its proponents argue that the dams provide flood control, irrigation, and more self- sufficiency in energy. Its opponents argue that the dams destroy valuable natural habitat and displace thousands of local people without adequate compensation. Other power sources are natural gas, coal, and oil. There are no operational nuclear power plants in the Philippines. The Bataan Nuclear Power Plant, completed in 1985, had its operations suspended in 1986 because of corruption charges, and in 1997 the government decided to convert the idle plant to a natural gas power plant. The Philippines continues to pursue the privatization of the state-owed National Power Company known as Napocor, but so far the initiative has been plagued by delays. Possible reasons include poor infrastructure and inflated valuations.

Services: The services sector, in which the Philippines apparently enjoys a comparative advantage, has grown steadily since 1985, when it accounted for about 40 percent of both gross domestic product (GDP) and the total number of persons employed. By 1999, services accounted for about 52 percent of GDP and about 45 percent of the total number of persons employed, and by 2004 those figures had risen to 53 percent and 48 percent, respectively. In the first half of 2005, the services sector grew more quickly (by 6.6. percent) than industry or agriculture. The fastest growing segments of the services sector were telecommunications, business outsourcing, and financial services.

Banking and Finance: The Central Bank of the Philippines supervises the nation's banking system. Nonbank financial intermediaries such as private insurance companies are overseen by the Insurance Commission and the Securities and Exchange Commission. The largest domestic banks, in order of size, are Metropolitan Bank and Trust (Metrobank), Bank of the Philippine Islands, Equitable-PCI Banking Corporation, Land Bank of the Philippines, Philippine National Bank, Development Bank of the Philippines, Rizal Commercial Banking Corporation, Banco de Oro, Allied Banking Corporation, and China Banking Corporation. There also are 32 other universal and commercial banks. Four of the banks are owned or controlled by the government: the Land Bank of the Philippines, the Philippine National Bank, the Development Bank of the Philippines, and the Al-Amanah Islamic Bank. In addition, the banking sector includes 93 thrift banks (savings and mortgage banks, stock savings and loan associations, private development banks, and micro-finance institutions) and 771 rural banks. The universal and commercial banks and the largest thrift banks have licences to operate foreign-currency deposit units. Foreign banks provide competition to local banks and are active in investment banking, asset management, and foreign-exchange and derivatives trading. Although they have a small market share and branch networks are not extensive, the expertise and reputation of the foreign banks attract customers.

The banking sector was relatively undamaged by the Asian financial crisis of 1997–98, and since 2001 asset quality has improved. In July 2005, nonperforming loans declined into the single digits (9.3 percent), half the peak level (18.8 percent) recorded in October 2001. This progress reflects the positive impact of the Special Purpose Vehicle Act of 2002, which provided incentives to financial institutions to reduce non-performing assets. Another trend in commercial banking is toward consolidation and restructuring.

The capitalization of the stock market is still modest, but it is growing rapidly off a low base. At the end of 2005, total stock market capitalization reached US$113 billion, up 25 percent from the previous year. During 2005, initial public offerings reached their highest level since the Asian financial crisis in 1997–98: US$1.06 billion. However, fewer than 1 percent of Filipinos invest in the stock market. Filipino investors generally prefer the bond market, which they regard as safer, and foreign investors also lack confidence in the stock market. The most important index, the Philippine Composite Index (PHISIX), consists of 34 listed issues, representing the country's most important companies. The main financial centers are in Manila, the location of the Philippine Stock Exchange, and in Cebu.

The Philippines had 34 life insurance firms in 2005; this number includes foreign insurers that dominate the industry. Three foreign-owned life insurers and four joint-venture (foreign and domestic) life insurers enjoyed a combined market share of about 60 percent. The Philippine American Life Insurance Company is the largest life insurance issuer with a market share of 23.6 percent.

Tourism: In 2005 about 2.6 million foreign tourists visited the Philippines—a record high. Tourists came from the following regions, listed in order of volume: East Asia, North America, Association of South East Asian

Nations, and Australiasia/Pacific. Authorities were hopeful that visitors could reach 3 million in 2006. Tourism has grown significantly since the first three years of the decade, when about 1.9 million foreigners visited the country each year. The Department of Tourism has actively promoted tourism to take advantage of the fact that the indirect impact of tourism on the economy is 2.5 times the actual money spent by visitors, according to a study by economists at the University of Asia and the Pacific. Prior to 2005, tourism had failed to flourish as a result of political and economic instability, the terrorist threat in the southern provinces, and the perception that other countries in the region offer better attractions. The Philippines is seeking more investment in hotels, restaurants, and other tourism-related infrastructure.

Labor: In December 2005, the unemployment rate was 7.4 percent, much lower than the roughly 11 percent average typical since the mid-1980s. The improvement was attributable to electronics exports, the end of drought conditions for agriculture, and growth in business outsourcing, real estate, and tourism. Some 32.9 million people were employed out of a total workforce of 35.5 million. However, the underemployment rate was 21.2 percent. In 2004 about 48 percent were employed in services, 36 percent in agriculture, and 16 percent in industry. Reflecting the lack of satisfactory employment opportunities at home, an estimated 652,000 Filipinos obtained employment outside the country as contract workers. About 4 million workers belong to trade unions, which are particularly prevalent in manufacturing. Labor relations generally are good because of the strict enforcement of labor laws and the acceptance of collective bargaining.

However, in 2003 some 38 new strikes, mostly attributable to unfair labor practices, led to the loss of 156,000 workdays, less than half the level in the previous year.

Foreign Economic Relations: The Philippines' foreign economic relations revolve around its Asian neighbors, with which it conducts a majority of its trade, and the United States, which is a major trading partner. The Philippines helped to found the Association of Southeast Asian Nations (ASEAN) in 1967. The Philippines also belongs to the Asia-Pacific Economic Cooperation (APEC) forum. ASEAN's goal of establishing a regional free-trade area has been only partially realized.

The Philippines has been a member of the World Trade Organization (WTO) since January 1, 1995. In 2001 the Philippine Bureau of International Trade Relations issued a positive assessment of the WTO's impact on the country's economic development. WTO membership has enabled the Philippines to adopt transparent trade rules regarding customs valuation, defenses against unfair trade, and protection of intellectual property rights. For example, in 1998 the government passed a law that improves the protection of intellectual property rights in the areas of copyrights, patents, and trademarks. However, the United States maintains that the intellectual property protections are inadequate and has taken initial steps toward imposing trade sanctions.

Imports: In 2004 the Philippines' imports were valued at US$45.1 billion, up 10.6 percent from the previous year. Principal imports were telecommunications and electronics equipment (34 percent), chemicals (7 percent), and crude petroleum (6 percent). The main origins of imports were Japan (19.8 percent), the United States (13.7 percent), China (7.7 percent), Singapore (7.4 percent), Taiwan (7.0 percent), and South Korea (5.6 percent).

Exports: In 2004 the Philippines' exports were valued at US$38.7 billion, up 9.6 percent from the previous year. Principal exports were electronic products (68.8 percent), clothing (5.6 percent), coconut oil (1.5 percent), and petroleum products (1.0 percent). Exported electronic products were primarily semiconductors. The main destinations of exports were Japan (20.1 percent), the United States (17.9 percent), the Netherlands (9.1 percent), Hong Kong (7.9 percent), China (6.7 percent), and Singapore (6.6 percent).

Trade Balance: In 2004 the Philippines incurred a merchandise trade deficit of US$6.4 billion, or 14 percent of imports. However, remittances of US$8.8 billion from Filipinos working overseas during 2004 more than offset the trade deficit. Such remittances surpassed US$10.8 billion in 2005. As recently as 2002, the Philippines had a slight trade surplus.

Balance of Payments: In 2004 the current account balance was US$2.1 billion. Since 1998, the Philippines has achieved a positive current account balance. Reflecting the sustained period of balance of payments surpluses, gross international reserves rose to a record US$18.6 billion in September 2005.

External Debt: In 2004 external debt amounted to US$61 billion, or 72.2 percent of gross domestic product (GDP).

Foreign Investment: In 2004 direct investment inflows were a modest US$57 million. Over the long term, direct and portfolio investment have been anemic, reflecting the relative unattractiveness of the economy, restrictions on foreign ownership, and the perception of political risk. The three top sources of foreign direct investment—ranked by amount—are the United States, Japan, and the Netherlands.

Currency and Exchange Rate: The currency is the Philippine peso (PHP). In mid-March 2006, the exchange rate was approximately PHP5 1 = US$1. The peso is made up of 100 centavos. Coins are issued in denominations of 1, 5, 10, and 25 centavos and 1, 5, and 10 pesos. Banknotes are issued in denominations ranging from 5 pesos to 1,000 pesos.

Fiscal Year: Calendar year.

TRANSPORTATION AND TELECOMMUNICATIONS

Overview: The transportation system faces the fundamental geographic challenge that the Philippines is a far-flung archipelago. This fact offers a partial explanation for the country's relatively undeveloped transportation infrastructure. Another reason is the sustained underinvestment in infrastructure since the 1997–98 Asian economic crisis. In 2003, for example, infrastructure investment accounted for only 3.6 percent of gross domestic product, well below the rate of investment in Thailand (15.4 percent) and Vietnam (9.9 percent). Consequently, the Philippines ranked 89 out of 102 countries in infrastructure quality in 2004, according to the World Economic Forum. Among developing economies in East Asia, the Philippines ranked last for the quality of its railroads, ports, and electrical systems. The road network is mostly unpaved, only slightly more than half of the limited railroad system is in operation, and only a few ports have major passenger and cargo terminals. President Gloria Macapagal-Arroyo hopes to establish a highway and ferry network that will ease travel across the archipelago.

Roads: Although an extensive road network covers almost the entire nation, the quality varies widely, and traffic congestion is common, particularly in Manila. Local governments are responsible for managing some 86 percent of the 202,000-kilometer network. An estimated 60 percent of roads are unpaved village roads. As for the national network, 70.4 percent of roads are paved with concrete or asphalt, with the remainder consisting of gravel or earth. In urban areas, transportation is available by car, bus, light rail, metro rail, and jeepney. The highly decorated but popular jeepney, a derivative of the World War II-era U.S. Army jeep, has been adapted to public transportation. In the provinces, buses, jeepneys, and three-wheeled taxis are the main modes of ground transportation. A priority in the nation's lagging road investment program is the improvement of roads carrying goods to and from ports.

Railroads: The Philippines has 897 kilometers of railroads, but much of the network in the north is closed because of its poor condition. The main railroad line, of which 440 kilometers are operational, is located on the island of Luzon, the largest island in the archipelago and home of Manila. On Luzon, the Philippine National Railways provides long-distance service, while in Metropolitan Manila, the Metro Rail Transit Authority and Light Rail Transit Authority provide elevated, light-rail service.

Ports: As an archipelago, the Philippines has more than 1,000 ports, of which 117 are regarded as international ports. The Philippines Port Authority, which administers the ports, has the mission of promoting maritime trade within the context of the Philippines' hoped-for transformation into a newly industrialized country. About 12 of the 117 international ports have major cargo and passenger terminals. The premier cargo terminal is in the Port of Manila. The domestic ports service inter-island boats, ferries, and roll-on, roll-off vessels. Some remote islands are accessible only by boat. In 2003 privately controlled ports accounted for 54 percent of total cargo serviced. Private ports generally handle more international trade, whereas government-run ports service mainly domestic trade.

Inland Waterways: The Philippines has 3,219 kilometers of inland waterways. The nation's inland waterway system is the thirty-second largest in the world.

Civil Aviation/Airports: The Philippines has 87 airports, including four major international airports: Mactan-Cebu International on Mactan Island in Cebu province, Ninoy Aquino International in Manila, Diosdado Macapagal International at the former U.S. Air Force base at Clark Field, north of Manila, and Davao International Airport near Davao City on Mindanao. Most of the other regional airports are substandard. The government is working on improving the civil aviation infrastructure. A legal dispute is holding up the opening of a newly constructed terminal at Ninoy Aquino International Airport. A consortium of international companies is seeking to recover investments in the project, following the revocation of the group's build-operate-transfer contract and seizure of the terminal by President Macapagal-Arroyo's administration. The government plans to complete the terminal in early 2006, but the opening is likely to be delayed. The flagship airline is Philippine Airlines, which serves 32 foreign and 21 domestic cities with a fleet of 30 Boeing and Airbus aircraft.

Pipelines: In October 2001, multinational energy companies began to tap natural gas from the Malampaya offshore field in the South China Sea by completing a 502-kilometer pipeline, one of the longest deep-water pipelines in the world. The Malampaya field is believed to contain 2.6 trillion cubic feet of natural gas. The natural gas will be used to fuel three power plants with a combined annual capacity of 2,700 megawatts.

Telecommunications: Mobile telecommunications are more popular than fixed-line telecommunications in the Philippines. An estimated 30–40 million Filipinos have cell phones. The Philippines uses the Global System for Mobile Communications, a second-generation digital technology employed by 71 percent of the world market. In November 2004, the National Telecommunications Commission held initial hearings to lay the groundwork for the introduction of third-generation digital technology, already widely used in the United States, Europe, and much of the Asia-Pacific region. In December 2005, the government authorized four domestic carriers to provide third-generation cellular service beginning in 2008. Third- generation technology enables high-speed, high-bandwidth video applications by cell phone. Currently, Short Message Service, a system for text messages under 160 characters in length, is widely used, with more than 200 million messages transmitted per day, but Multimedia Message Service has been gaining acceptance since its introduction in 2003.

In 2003 the Philippines had 11.5 million radios, 3.7 million televisions, and 1.5 million personal computers. Internet access is modest, particularly in comparison to other countries in the region. Whereas South Korea boasts the world's highest Internet broadband penetration rate, only about 5 million Filipinos have Internet access, and 85 percent of them rely on dial-up connections. The Philippine Long Distance Company, the largest telecommunications provider, is responsible for maintaining a national digital fiber-optic network, digital microwave radio, and satellite communications.

Government and Politics

Overview: In February 1987, the Philippines adopted a new constitution that instituted the presidential-style republican form of democracy, which resembles the U.S. model much more than the European parliamentary system. One key difference between the Philippine and U.S. systems is that the Philippines is a unitary republic, whereas the United States is a federal republic, with significant powers reserved for the states. In the Philippines, by contrast, the national government is not challenged by local authority. The ratification of the 1987 constitution—the fourth in the nation's history—by national referendum signaled the country's return to democracy following the autocratic rule of Fernando Marcos (1965–86). Politics in the Philippines is somewhat tumultuous. In February 2006, the president declared a state of emergency after quashing the attempted coup staged by the political opposition.

Executive Branch: Embracing the concept of separation of powers, the constitution provides for a president, who is simultaneously head of government and chief of state, a separately elected vice president, a bicameral legislature, and an independent judiciary. The constitution includes legislative and judicial limits on the power of the president. The president cannot abolish Congress, and Congress can override a presidential veto with a two-thirds majority vote. Moreover, the president needs Congressional support in order to implement policies and programs. The Supreme Court rules on the constitutionality of presidential decrees.

The president is elected to a single six-year term by direct universal suffrage; the vice president may be elected to a maximum of two consecutive six-year terms. The vice president may be appointed to the cabinet without legislative confirmation. The current president is Gloria Macapagal-Arroyo, who originally took office in January 2001, when she succeeded Joseph Estrada following his impeachment in November 2000. In May 2004, Macapagal-Arroyo was elected to a full term. The vice president, since June 2004, is Noli de Castro. The executive functions of the government are carried out through the Cabinet of Ministers. The cabinet, which in 2005 consisted of heads of 22 departments and offices, is appointed by the president with the consent of the Commission of Appointments.

Legislative Branch: The bicameral Congress of the Philippines consists of the Senate (upper chamber) and House of Representatives (lower chamber). Members of the 24-seat Senate are elected at large to six-year terms and are limited to no more than two consecutive terms. The current president of the Senate (since 2000) is Franklin M. Drilon. The House is limited by the constitution to no more than 250 members. In 2005 there were 238 members, of whom 214 (80 percent) were elected for three-year terms from legislative districts apportioned among the provinces, cities, and the Metropolitan Manila area in accordance with the population, on the basis of a uniform and progressive ratio. The other 24 members (limited by the constitution to 20 percent of the total) are presidential appointees elected through a party-list system of registered national, regional, and sectoral parties or organizations. House members are limited to no more than three consecutive terms. The current speaker of the House (now in his third term as speaker, most recently since 2004) is José de Venecia. By means of a two-thirds majority vote, Congress can override presidential vetoes and declare a state of war.

Judicial Branch: The Philippines has an independent judiciary, with the Supreme Court as the highest court of appeal. The Supreme Court also is empowered to review the constitutionality of presidential decrees. The Supreme Court consists of a chief justice and 14 associate justices. It is not necessary for the entire court to convene in all cases. Justices are appointed by the president on the recommendation of the Judicial and Bar Council and serve until 70 years of age. The current chief justice, since 1998, is Hilario G. Davide, Jr. Lower-level courts include a national Court of Appeals divided into 17 divisions, local and regional trial courts, and an informal local system to settle certain disputes outside the formal court system. In 1985 a separate court system founded on Islamic law (sharia) was established in the southern Philippines with jurisdiction over family and contractual relations among Muslims. Three district magistrates and six circuit judges oversee the Islamic law system. A special court—the Sandiganbayan or anti-graft court— focuses exclusively on investigating charges of judicial corruption.

Administrative Divisions: Administrative divisions consist of regions, provinces, chartered cities, municipalities, and *barangays* (villages). Chartered cities are not part of any province and do not elect provincial officials. The

Philippines has 17 regions, 79 provinces, 117 chartered cities, 1,500 municipalities, and 41,975 *barangays*. Metropolitan Manila, which is regarded as a region, consists of 14 cities, 3 municipalities, and 1,694 *barangays*. The Autonomous Region in Muslim Mindanao was established in 1990 following a plebicite in late 1989.

Provincial and Local Government: Governors and vice governors are elected to head provinces, the largest local administrative unit. Appointed functionaries responsible for managing offices concerned with finance, tax collection, audit, public works, agricultural services, health, and schools are subordinate not just to the governor, but also to national ministries. Because the Philippines is a unitary republic, local government has less power than it would have in a federal system. In fact, according to the constitution, the president oversees local government. The single biggest problem for local government has been inadequate funding. Although local government is permitted to levy taxes, such taxes are subject to restrictions by Congress, and they have been difficult to collect in practice. A fragmented four-province Autonomous Region in Muslim Mindanao was formally established in November 1990 with its own governor and unicameral legislature.

Judicial and Legal System: The basis of the legal code is primarily Spanish and Anglo- American law. Islamic law applies among Muslims in portions of the southern Philippines. According to the constitution, those accused of crimes have the right to be informed of the charges against them, to be represented by counsel, and to have a speedy and fair public trial. Defendants also enjoy the presumption of innocence and have the right to confront witnesses, present evidence, and appeal convictions. However, the judiciary is said to suffer from corruption and inefficiency, which at times undermine the provision of due process and equal justice. As a result, the Supreme Court has undertaken a five-year program to speed up the judicial process and crack down on corruption.

Electoral System: The Philippines has universal direct suffrage at age 18 and older to elect the president, vice president (who runs independently), and most of the seats in the bicameral legislature, consisting of the House of Representatives and the Senate; a minority of House members known as sectoral representatives are appointed by the president. Elections are held not just for national leadership but also for representation at the provincial and local levels. In the last elections in May 2004, some 74 percent of eligible voters participated, but the process was marred by violence and numerous irregularities, which the political opposition continues to protest, even calling for the president's impeachment.

Politics and Political Parties: President Macapagal-Arroyo represents the conservative LakasChristian Muslim Democratic Party (Lakas-CMD), since the May 2004 election the largest faction in the House of Representatives (100 seats). Lakas-CMD has formed a governing coalition with the Liberal Party (32 seats). Others parties in the House are the Nationalist Peoples Coalition (47 seats); Struggle for Democratic Filipinos (nine seats); Nationalista Party (six seats); Akbayan (three seats); Association of Philippine Electric Co-operatives (three seats); Bayan Muna (three seats); Power of the Filipino Masses (three seats); Aksyon Demokratiko, Promdi, and Reporma, which have formed an alliance (two seats); Philippine Democratic Party (two seats); and Philippines Democratic Socialist Party (two seats). Personalities are more important than parties in Philippine politics. Movie stars and other celebrities have enjoyed considerable success. In addition, several prominent families play a disproportionate role in politics.

Mass Media: The Office of the President is responsible for managing the government's policy toward the press, but freedom of speech and freedom of the press are enshrined in the 1987 constitution. Although independent observers credit the government with respecting freedom of the press in general, the government has been criticized for failing to investigate thoroughly summary killings of journalists and for subjecting journalists to harassment and surveillance. The most widely read newspapers are the *Manila Bulletin*, *Philippine Star*, *Philippine Daily Inquirer*, *Manila Times*, and *Business World*. In 2004 the country had 225 television stations, 369 AM radio broadcast stations, 583 FM radio broadcast stations, and 5 shortwave stations. Although some media outlets, such as IBC (television) and the Philippine Broadcasting Service (radio), are government-run, most outlets are privately owned. Much media ownership is concentrated in the hands of prominent families and businesses. Consequently, some reports tend to be one-sided presentations favoring special interests. The privately owned press also tends toward sensationalism at times.

Foreign Relations: The foreign policy of the Philippines aims to promote democracy and human rights and the welfare of some 7 million overseas workers. The Philippines maintains close ties to Persian Gulf and other Middle

Eastern nations where many of these workers are employed. In an effort to expand its relationship with the Islamic world, the Philippines is seeking observer status in the Organization of the Islamic Conference. The Philippines is an active member of the Association of Southeast Asian Nations. The Philippines also has participated in a variety of United Nations-sponsored peacekeeping missions. However, in July 2004, after a Filipino truck driver was taken hostage in Iraq, the Philippines elected to withdraw troops from that embattled nation in order to win his release.

The Philippines maintains strong ties to the United States, which designated the nation a major non-North Atlantic Treaty Organization ally in 2003. Although the United States mildly rebuked the Philippines for yielding to insurgent demands in Iraq to withdraw its small contingent, the United States continues to view the Philippines as an important ally in the war on terrorism, particularly in view of various Islamic insurgencies on the islands of Mindanao and Jolo. The relationship with the United States was redefined in the early 1990s, when the United States complied with Philippine demands to vacate various military bases, including the naval base at Subic Bay. However, the two nations remain close, and in May 2004 the Philippines signed an agreement with the United States exempting U.S. military personnel in the Philippines from prosecution before the International Criminal Court.

The Philippines has an improving, but still fragile, relationship with China. As reflected in President Macapagal-Arroyo's visit to China in 2001, the Philippines is seeking closer economic cooperation with China, even as it fears China's growing economic and military clout. A territorial dispute over control of the Spratly Islands in the South China Sea is an impediment to better relations. China also is concerned about the Philippines' strong ties to the United States, which it views as a strategic rival in the region.

The Philippines cooperates with the neighboring countries of Indonesia and Malaysia in combating the regional threat posed by the Islamic terrorist group Jemaah Islamiyah. Relations with Indonesia improved following the ouster of President Suharto in May 1998 after 32 years of authoritarian rule. Suharto's overthrow mirrored Ferdinand Marcos's overthrow in the Philippines in 1986. The Philippines' relations with Malaysia are somewhat impaired by a territorial dispute over the state of Sabah, which is now part of Malaysia.

Japan and the United States are the Philippines' leading trading partners and sources of direct investment. Japan is the top source of development assistance. Australia also is a significant economic and security partner. The Philippines and Singapore share a close economic and political relationship with the United States, and the two nations have engaged in joint military training exercises.

Membership in International Organizations: The Philippines belongs to the United Nations (UN), the World Trade Organization, and several key Asian regional organizations, notably the Association of Southeast Asian Nations (ASEAN), ASEAN's Regional Forum, the Asian Development Bank, and the Asia Pacific Economic Cooperation (APEC) forum. In addition, the Philippines is a member of the following international organizations: Colombo Plan, Customs Cooperation Council, Group of 24, Group of 77, International Chamber of Commerce, International Confederation of Free Trade Unions, International Criminal Police Organization, International Federation of Red Cross and Red Crescent Societies, International Hydrographic Organization, International Olympic Committee, International Organization for Migration, International Organization for Standardization, Non-Aligned Movement, Organisation for the Prohibition of Chemical Weapons, World Confederation of Labor, World Federation of Trade Unions, and World Tourism Organization. The Philippines has applied for observer status in the Organization of the Islamic Conference.

During 2004–5 the Philippines served as a temporary member of the UN Security Council. The Philippines is a permanent member of the following UN-affiliated organizations: Economic and Social Commission for Asia and the Pacific, Food and Agriculture Organization, International Atomic Energy Agency, International Bank for Reconstruction and Development (World Bank), International Civil Aviation Organization, International Development Association, International Finance Corporation, International Fund for Agricultural Development, International Labour Organization, International Maritime Organization, International Monetary Fund, International Telecommunication Union, UN Conference on Aid and Development, UN Educational, Scientific and Cultural Organization, UN Industrial Development Organization, UN Office of the High Commissioner for Refugees, UN University, Universal Postal Union, World Health Organization, World Intellectual Property Organization, and World Meteorological Organization.

Major International Treaties: The Philippines is a party to the following environmental agreements: Biodiversity, Climate Change, Climate Change-Kyoto Protocol, Desertification, Endangered Species, Hazardous Wastes, Law of the Sea, Marine Dumping, Ozone Layer Protection, Ship Pollution, Tropical Timber 83, Tropical Timber 94, Wetlands, and Whaling. The Philippines has signed, but not ratified, the agreement on Air Pollution-Persistent Organic Pollutants. In the area of arms control, the Philippines is a party to the Biological Weapons Convention, Chemical Weapons Convention, Treaty on the Non-Proliferation of Nuclear Weapons, and Limited Test Ban Treaty. The Philippines has ratified numerous international human rights agreements, including those against slavery, genocide, prisoner of war abuse, human trafficking, racial discrimination, and torture. The Philippines also has adopted agreements designed to protect women, children, and refugees. Although the Philippines is a member of the World Intellectual Property Organization (WIPO), it has not ratified the WIPO Performances and Phonograms Treaty or the Copyright Treaty.

NATIONAL SECURITY

Armed Forces Overview: The Armed Forces of the Philippines (AFP) consists of a 66,000- member army; a 24,000-member navy, including 7,500 marines; and a 16,000-member air force. Active forces are supplemented by 131,000 reserves. A joint service command covers five military areas. The 6,000-member National Capital Region Command, established in November 2003, is responsible for protecting the government against coup attempts. The president of the republic is commander in chief of the armed forces. The AFP is poorly funded and is armed with antiquated equipment. In 2003 the government moved to replace World War II-era rifles. In addition, only slightly more than half of the Philippines' naval ships are operational, and only a few air force planes are combat ready. Compounding the problem of inadequate equipment, the AFP's leadership has been accused of corruption and complicity with insurgent groups, although its primary mission involves counterinsurgency. In July 2003, junior officers staged an unsuccessful coup. The Philippines is the recipient of U.S. military assistance.

Foreign Military Relations: The United States and the Philippines have a mutual defense treaty that has been in effect since 1952, but it does not extend to territorial disputes involving the Spratly Islands. In 2003 the United States designated the Philippines as a major non-North Atlantic Treaty Organization ally. Total U.S. military assistance to the Philippines rose from US$38 million in 2001 to US$114 million in 2003 and a projected US$164 million in 2005, which would make the Philippines the fourth largest recipient of U.S. foreign military assistance. Australia reportedly also a major source of military assistance.

External Threat: The Philippines faces no major external threat.

Defense Budget: The defense budget for 2005 totaled US$840 million, or 5 percent of the proposed government budget of US$16.5 billion. Almost half of the defense budget was designated for the army. Viewed another way, 80 percent of the budget was slated for personnel and almost the entire remaining amount, for maintenance and operating expenses. Thus, less than 1 percent was available for desperately needed procurement.

Major Military Units: The army has eight light infantry divisions, one special operations command, five engineering battalions, one artillery regiment at headquarters, one presidential security group, and three light-reaction companies. The navy has two commands—Fleet and Marine Corps. Navy bases are located at Sangley Point/Cavite, Zamboanga, and Cebu. The air force is organized into headquarters and five commands: air defense, tactical operations, air education and training, air logistics and supply, and air reserves.

Major Military Equipment: The army is equipped with 65 light tanks, 85 armored infantry fighting vehicles, and 370 armored personnel carriers, as well as towed artillery, mortars, recoilless launchers, and several small aircraft. The navy is equipped with one frigate; 58 patrol and coastal combatants; 7 amphibious ships, plus about 39 amphibious craft; and 11 support and miscellaneous vessels. However, in April 2003 the armed forces chief of staff stated that only 56 percent of the navy's vessels were operational. Naval aviation has six transport aircraft and four search-and-rescue helicopters. The air force has 36 combat aircraft and 25 armed helicopters.

Military Service: The Armed Forces of the Philippines (AFP) is an all-volunteer force. The minimum age for service is 20 years.

Paramilitary Forces: Paramilitary forces include the civilian Philippine National Police (under the Department of Interior and Local Government), with an estimated 115,000 personnel; the Coast Guard (run by the navy but technically part of the Department of Transportation and Communications), numbering 3,500; and local citizen armed militias, the Civilian Armed Forces Geographical Units (CAFGUs) estimated to number 40,000–82,000.

Foreign Military Forces: Beginning in 2002, the U.S. military has assisted the Armed Forces of the Philippines in fighting the Abu Sayyaf Group (ASG), an al Qaeda affiliate. Although foreign militaries are formally banned from conducting operations on Philippine soil, the U.S. military has maintained an officially advisory presence in the Philippines continuously since 2002. The two nations regularly conduct joint training exercises in the Philippines.

Military Forces Abroad: The Philippines has participated in a variety of United Nations (UN)- sponsored peacekeeping missions, most recently the UN Mission in Burundi, the UN Mission of Support in East Timor, the UN Stabilization Mission in Haiti, the UN Mission in Ivory Coast, and the UN Mission in Liberia. The Philippines also participated in United States-led operations in Iraq, with troops involved in humanitarian assistance starting in August 2003. However, the Philippines decided to withdraw its small force in July 2004 when insurgents took a Filipino truck driver hostage.

Police: The Department of Interior and Local Government oversees the Philippine National Police (PNP), which has an active force of about 115,000. The PNP, which had been entrusted with internal security in 1996, lost this role two years later, when the Armed Forces of the Philippines—particularly the army—reasserted its lead role in internal security. In September 2002, the PNP regained some of its authority when it was allowed to form a counterinsurgency task force in northeast Mindanao. Meanwhile, the army established a parallel task force in southwest Mindanao.

Internal Threat: Insurgencies by various Islamic terrorist and separatist groups and the communist New People's Army pose a significant internal threat. In response to this situation and the global war on terrorism, the Armed Forces of the Philippines (AFP) has been restructured to combat domestic insurgencies, most of which are based on the southern island of Mindanao: the Moro Islamic Liberation Front (MILF), the Abu Sayyaf Group (ASG), Jemaah Islamiyah, and the Communist Party of the Philippines' New People's Army (NPA). In addition, the loyalty of the military to the government remains in doubt, following an unsuccessful coup by a renegade faction of the AFP in July 2003.

Terrorism: The Philippines faces an indigenous terrorist threat from several organizations: the Moro Islamic Liberation Front (MILF), the Abu Sayyaf Group (ASG), Jemaah Islamiyah (JI), and the communist New People's Army (NPA). The MILF and ASG, which aspire to establish an Islamic state on Mindanao, are reputed to have links to al Qaeda. The MILF, which has engaged in sporadic peace negotiations with the government and has some moderate elements, is the largest of the groups, with about 10,000 to 11,000 soldiers. The more militant ASG, after being forced to abandon its stronghold on the island of Basilan by the Armed Forces of the Philippines, has regrouped on Jolo. About 400 guerrillas now are affiliated with the group, about half the original level before its confrontation with the Philippine military. Jemaah Islamiyah, an al Qaeda affiliate active in Indonesia but with branches across Southeast Asia, allegedly failed to execute plans to bomb ceremonies marking the inauguration of the new Philippine government in June 2004. The NPA, the military wing of the Communist Party of the Philippines, has about 3,000 guerrillas on Mindanao.

Human Rights: According to a U.S. Department of State report released in March 2006, Philippine security forces have been responsible for serious human rights abuses despite the efforts of civilian authorities to control them. The report found that although the government generally respected human rights, some security forces elements—particularly the Philippine National Police—practiced extrajudicial killings, vigilantism, disappearances, torture, and arbitrary arrest and detention in their battle against criminals and terrorists. Prison conditions were harsh, and the slow judicial process as well as corrupt police, judges, and prosecutors impaired due process and the rule of law. Besides criminals and terrorists, human rights activists, left-wing political activists, and Muslims were sometimes the victims of improper police conduct. Violence against women and abuse of children remained serious problems, and some children were pressed into slave labor and prostitution.

INDEX

A

B

C

D

E

F

J

K

L

M

N

O

P

Q

R

S